The Battle of Edgcote

1469

Re-evaluating the evidence

By Graham Evans

Published by the Northamptonshire Battlefields Society

First published 2019 by the Northamptonshire Battlefields Society

© Northamptonshire Battlefields Society 2019

All rights reserved. No part of this book may be reprinted or reproduced or utilised in any form or by any electronic, mechanical or other means, now known or hereafter invented, including photocopying or in any information storage or retrieval system, without the written permission of the author.

Graham Evans has asserted his moral right to be identified as the author of this work, and in accordance with the Copyrights, Design and Patents Act 1988.

Cover photograph © Mike Ingram

ISBN 9781794611078

Acknowledgements

Whilst the physical writing of a book is a solo endeavour with the author bathed in the glow of an electronic screen it can only come about with the support of many people. The Northamptonshire Battlefields Society groups together a number of enthusiastic people who care deeply for their county's heritage. The Chairman, Mike Ingram, and most notably fellow member, Phil Steele, have been at the fore front of promoting the importance of Edgcote in the run up to the 550th anniversary year, and they both have my deepest thanks for their assistance in getting my thoughts straight. Indeed, without both of them this would never have been written.

The text was very kindly read for me and commented on by Jenny Rose, another stalwart of the Society, and also Ian Drury who has considerably more knowledge about how to put such a book together than I do. I can only thank all of them for selflessly giving of their time to help with a book on such an obscure piece of medieval military history.

Finally I must acknowledge the help and support of my wife, Heather, who has not only put up with me endlessly discussing the various theories that have made it into the final version of this book with good humour, but also read the final text as well, and is a constant reminder that I shouldn't take myself too seriously.

And yes, I will have a cup of tea, thank you.

Contents

Introduction	1
Chapter 1 - A Tale of Two Historians	4
Chapter 2 - A Lack of Sources?	9
Chapter 3 - The Numbers Game	15
Chapter 4 - Location, Location, Location	29
Chapter 5 - Naming the Day	44
Chapter 6 - "I am Robin of Redesdale!"	49
Chapter 7 - The Most Mighty Battlefield	57
Chapter 8 - Retribution and Reckoning	77
Chapter 9 - Aftermath and Afterthoughts	84
Appendix - Primary Sources	87
Bibliography	136
The Battlefield Today	139
Northamptonshire Battlefields Society	141

Maps and Illustrations

Main locations in the 1469 Campaign	3
Title Page "Lancaster & York" by Sir James H Ramsey	5
Title Page "Hall's Chronicle"	6
Title Page "Coventry Leet Book"	10
Map of Edgcote from "Lancaster & York"	35
Banbury Lane today	37
Edgcote Lodge Hill, looking north	38
The "West Hill" seen from the "East Hill"	42
The "East Hill" from Danes Moor	42
Map of alternative location theories	43
The Battlefield Trust information board at Edgcote	44
Parsons Street, Banbury, today	65
The Battle of Edgcote, Phase 1	69
The Battle of Edgcote, Phase 2	70
The Battle of Edgcote, Phase 3	71
The Battle of Edgcote, Phase 4	72

Picture Credits

The illustrations on pages 5, 6, 10, and 35 are taken from the respective publications on the Archive.org website, a most valuable resource, particularly for publications that are now out of copyright.

All other photographs and maps © Graham Evans, except where noted.

Introduction

The reason for this book is quite simple. 2019 is the 550th anniversary of the Battle of Edgcote fought in South Northamptonshire, just across the county boundary from Banbury. It seemed appropriate therefore that Northamptonshire Battlefields Society's "Edgcote 550" project should plan to publish a book on the battle, along with its other aims such as a battlefield model, a leaflet for walkers and a commemorative conference/study day. Edgcote is a little regarded battle in comparison to the overall impact its outcome had on the ruling classes of Wales and England. Had it turned out differently the readeption of Henry VI would probably never have happened and the battles of Barnet and Tewkesbury might never have been fought.

The first pedantic point to make is that whilst the battle takes place in the period we call the Wars of the Roses, it isn't a Wars of the Roses battle. You will look in vain for the Lancastrian interest in either army. This campaign could easily be termed "The Yorkist Civil War" or "Warwick's Rebellion", and it forced the ruling Yorkist group to take sides, either for the King or his over-mighty subject.

The immediate impact of the battle was felt outside the borders of Northamptonshire. In practice the county merely provided a location for forces from the North and South West of England, Wales and perhaps Kent or Calais to fight a battle, although it is possible a small number of locals may have intervened at the end to settle the day. Regardless of the number of men involved the casualty role was not inconsiderable, and they deserve more than the cursory line or two the battle usually warrants in a general history of the period.

This book will contain a narrative of the campaign and battle, but it is hoped to go further than that. There has been no full study of the battle for more than two decades[1], and those findings were, to some extent, controversial. The Battlefields Trust accepts that there are difficulties with understanding the battle, and the entry on the Resources Centre of their website is very detailed in some areas in order to explain its conclusions as to the battle's location.

None of this has stopped battlefield enthusiasts from walking the field, - it is one of three battles connected by the Battlefield Trail which was sponsored by the Battlefields Trust - and marking the yearly anniversary. It was on one of the anniversary walks, on a surprisingly chilly July evening that was more autumnal than summery, when a detailed discussion took place between those on the walk about what the sources actually told us about the battle. Frankly it did not seem to me that it all added up as it should, and the sense I got around me was that others were of the same view. On returning home it didn't take me long to realise that the way sources were being used was not necessarily appropriate, and that cross checking of assertions and assumptions was essential. Whilst it is not the intent to litter this book with footnotes, I have tried

---

[1] Philip Haigh's book "Where both the hosts fought" which covers both Edgcote and Losecote was published in 1997.

where possible to support all statements of fact with appropriate references, and hopefully made clear when I am speculating on what may have happened.

As the Society started to put together its Edgcote 550 project Phil Steele and I prepared an evening's presentation for the membership that looked at why the battle was fought where it was and also, crucially, what the sources told us and how they related to one another. The work I did on the sources for this talk ended up providing the framework for Chapter 2 of this book. It was also clear, as I worked through all of them that they didn't necessarily say what historians wanted them to say, which has lead to Chapter 1's discussion of the defining works in the historiography of the battle. I have also included reprints in the original format where ever possible of all of the primary sources used in the book, together with new translations of relevant materials. References to these are not, generally speaking, footnoted as the reader can turn to the back of the book to check up on me.

One of the biggest issues that we had with trying to interpret the battle was in determining how many people were involved. The numbers in the sources are massively inconsistent, and most historians plump for a number with little background as to why the number is a good or bad one. We have therefore, as a group, gone into the sizing of late medieval armies in quite a lot of detail, and the results are included in Chapter 3, - although the conclusions are my own, and no one else in the Society is to blame for them.

With this as background, the tone and approach when preparing this book has resulted in something that is part narrative history, part explanatory lecture and part the sort of argument you might get in a pub between well informed history undergraduates[2]. Some of it may even border on the polemical. What it is hoped is that should anyone wish to write about Edgcote in the future they will find this book a useful starting point and guide to what could have happened, what may have happened and what didn't happen.

---

[2] At least we had arguments like this when I was an undergraduate, - times may have changed.

Main locations in 1469 Campaign

Chapter 1 - A Tale of Two Historians

Historians do not work in isolation. Regardless of how the individual might try, any work is coloured by the work of the historians who have gone before us, and anyone who reads a history book will set their understanding in the context of what they already know. What that means is that in order to do a re-evaluation of the Battle of Edgcote, it is helpful to look at the accepted interpretation, and why that interpretation tends to hold sway.

This is not to say that historians and historical writers have not revisited the evidence or provided variations on the normal interpretation. However, it is certainly the case that two historians have influenced very strongly all subsequent interpretations. It is not the intention to undermine the value of either piece of work, but their pivotal influence in the historiography of the subject has to be recognised. Each historian builds on the work that has gone before - even in a work like this - and we have to recognise that our understanding of the past evolves, with each generation building on the past.

So it is that we need to recognise the importance in our understanding of the work done by Edward Hall (1497 - 1547) and Sir James Ramsay (1832 - 1925).

To start with the most recent first. The late 19th Century was blessed with a number of historians of considerable status. Amongst their number were Sir Charles Oman, the military historian, Samuel Gardiner, the historian of the English Civil War and the Puritan Revolution, Sir Charles Firth, who with T F Tout did so much to promote "scientific" history, and Sir James Ramsay of Banff, the 10th Baronet, author of "Lancaster and York, A Century of English History 1399 – 1485". They were a community who shared research, - most notably in the case of Gardiner and Firth, but also most likely Ramsay and Oman[1]. In respect to the 15th Century Ramsay's book is a work of enormous scholarship, and he is one of our most important medieval historians.

Ramsay's book, published in 1892, is very influential. Although subsequently superseded it laid the foundation in terms of identifying sources and creating the chronology of the period. It is likely that anyone taught the history of the Wars of the Roses in the first half of the 20th century will have been taught from a narrative derived from Ramsay, and those who studied the same period in the second half by those who learned from him.

Ramsay's account of the Edgcote campaign and battle, however, relies very heavily on the second of our two historians, one from a much earlier period.

The Tudor historian, Edward Hall, wrote his monumental "Chronicle" or "The Union of the Two Noble and Illustrate Famelies of Lancaster and Yorke" in the latter part of the reign of Henry VIII. Although Hall saw himself as a historian the tendency

---

[1] Oman also wrote a biography of Warwick, called "Warwick the Kingmaker" published in 1891, at the same time Ramsay was working on "Lancaster & York". It is a stimulating read, but completely devoid of any references or a bibliography.

has been to regard him as a primary source. It is alleged that he provided the main source material for Shakespeare's history plays.[2] Those who are deeply involved in defending the reputation of Richard of Gloucester frequently accuse Hall of being subject to, or the purveyor of, Tudor propaganda but that does not prevent any student of the period at some point going to Hall for understanding as to what was happening.

When considering the campaign and battle of Edgcote, Hall is very attractive as a source for a number of reasons. Firstly, he was well connected, and may have had access to the descendants of those who took part in the battle. Secondly, his account is the most comprehensive of all of the early accounts. Thirdly, he has an eye for detail and salacious tit-bits, which elevate his work above a mere chronicle of events. On the down side he was writing during the reign of a Tudor King, whose legitimacy depended upon your view of history, so the wise antiquarian trod carefully.

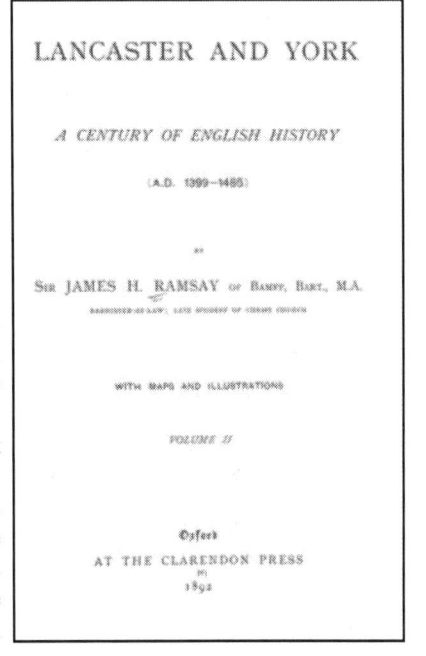

Of course, Hall is not relied upon exclusively in Ramsay's account, which also makes frequent reference to Warkworth, Polydore Vergil and other contemporary sources,[3] but it does provide the general framework for the account.

Following Ramsay there has developed a general consensus of what happened, when, where and why. The background to the campaign was the Earl of Warwick's increasing dissatisfaction with his role in court and his declining influence over Edward IV due to the rise of the latter's wife's family, the Woodvilles, headed by Lord Rivers.

Warwick was assisted in his ambitions by Edward's disaffected brother, George, Duke of Clarence. Although Edward had fathered three children with Elizabeth Woodville by 1469 in five years of marriage (a pretty good hit rate by anyone's reckoning), all of them were girls. Should Edward die without further issue, George was in a good position to succeed to the throne. His nose was particularly put out of joint by his brother's refusal to sanction his marriage to Isabel Neville, Warwick's daughter and eldest child. This led to a notable act of defiance when he went to Calais to be married to her, in a ceremony on the 11th July performed by Warwick's brother George Neville, who was the Archbishop of York.

---
[2] If he did then the Bard of Avon overlooked Edgcote completely.
[3] An analysis of the merits or otherwise of the various primary sources is given below in Chapter 2, and relevant extracts from the source texts are reprinted in an Appendix at the end of the book.

Meanwhile Warwick had been making arrangements for a coup d'état. The North of England was fertile ground for rebellion, and 1469 was a year when several broke out. An initial rebellion, lead by Robin of Holderness, in opposition to the abuse of charitable gifts by a hospital in York, was not sanctioned by Warwick, and was suppressed by his brother, John Neville, the Earl of Northumberland. It was followed shortly after, however, by a more serious outbreak, led by the mysterious "Robin of Redesdale" who is normally identified as Sir John Conyers, either father or son.

These rebels proclaimed a manifesto condemning the King's councillors on the grounds that they were insufficiently noble to be accorded the honour of advising him and holding lucrative jobs. The manifesto specifically named the Woodvilles, Sir William Herbert the Earl of Pembroke, Sir Humphrey Stafford the Earl of Devon,[4] and Lord Audley, and effectively demanded a return to the good old days, when the Earl of Warwick was one of his chief councillors. The manifesto makes reference to Edward II, Richard II, and Henry VI, all of whom, it said did exclude "gret lordis of thayre blood from thaire secrete Councelle". Having stated their aims, they formed up and marched south.

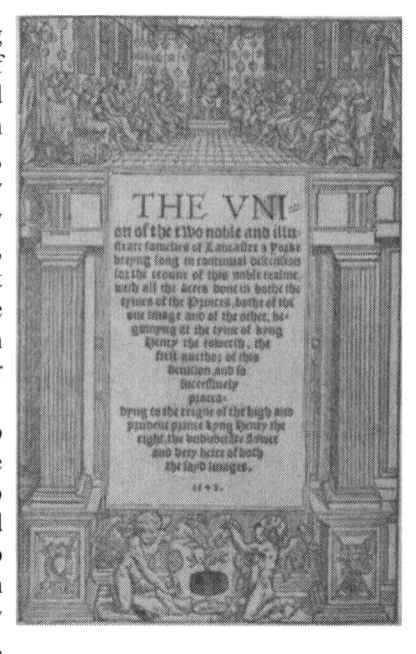

Edward was aware of difficulties in the North, but took a leisurely approach to dealing with them, going on a perambulation round the East Midlands and East Anglia in June and July. He was becoming concerned about the activities of Warwick and Clarence, and summoned Pembroke and Stafford to march to him with all their strength. Warwick and Clarence were now back in England, marching through Kent, gathering their supporters.

Whilst Edward dallied in Nottingham, Robin of Redesdale slipped past him, headed for a rendezvous with Warwick in the vicinity of Northampton. Pembroke and Stafford, having met up in the Cotswolds, were also moving towards Northampton with the aim of eventually meeting up with Edward, presumably just south of Nottingham.

The outriders from the Pembroke/Devon force and those from the rebels ran into one another around Northampton, - under a woodside, it is reported in Hall – when Pembroke's men tried to ambush the rebels' rear guard. Based on other evidence in

---

[4] Stafford is also sometimes referred to as Baron Stafford of Southwick/Southwyck as he was only created Earl of Devon in early 1469.

the sources the late Victorian writers determined this fight took place at Daventry[5] on the 25th July

Pembroke's men fell back down the main road to Banbury (now the A361), past Byfield, and back to their main force, followed by the rebels. Not all was well in the Royalist camp, however, notwithstanding this surprising rebuff. Pembroke & Stafford had fallen out over who should have a certain set of lodgings in Banbury. As Hall puts it: "there the erle of Pembroke, putte the Lorde Stafforde out of an Inne wherein he delighted muche to be, for the loue of a damosell that dwelled in the house". This story, in modern tellings, is known as "The Banbury Barmaid" incident.

Not only had they fallen out, but Stafford actually withdrew his part of the army, which included all of the force's archers.

Skirmishing between the outriders of both armies continued, and a clash led to the rebel captain, Sir Henry Neville, Lord Latimer's son, being captured, and summarily done to death by the Welshmen.

When the battle opened on the following day, the 26th July,[6] Pembroke was occupying a hill top position which can be identified from Hall's description as being the hill on which Edgcote Lodge Farm now sits. He was forced off this strong position by the rebel archers, as he had none with which to reply in kind, due to Stafford's leaving the day before. Charging down into the Northerners, the Welsh engaged the rebels,[7] and were gaining the upper hand, due to the martial prowess of Pembroke's brother, Sir Richard Herbert, who twice fought his way into the enemy formation and returned unharmed.

However, the tide turned when the cries of "A Warwick! A Warwick!" were heard, and rebel forces in the Earl of Warwick's red livery marching beneath his White Bear banner, emerged on the flank or rear of the Royalists, causing them to break and flee. What then followed was a massive slaughter of the nobility of South Wales, as they fled towards the River Cherwell and their homeland. Local tradition has it that many of them were killed at the river crossing where Trafford Bridge now stands.

In fact, the reinforcements were nothing but a hastily cobbled together force consisting, according to Hall, of "CCCCC [500] men gathered of all the Rascal of the towne of Northampton and other villages about". They were led by John Clapham, a servant to the Earl of Warwick. Notwithstanding their poor provenance and the element of bluff involved they were devastatingly effective.

The effect on Welsh nobility was catastrophic, with 168 Welshmen of consequence amongst the fallen. Quarter was not given in retribution for the ignoble slaying of Sir

---

[5] Ramsay, Lancaster & York p340, Oman, Warwick the Kingmaker p186.
[6] Hall says "The erle of Penbroke and the lorde Stafford of Southwike, wer lodged at Banbery the daie before the feld whiche was sainct Iames daie". St James Day is the 25th July.
[7] Most modern writers diverge from Ramsay here, believing the fighting took place on Danes Moor, whereas Ramsay places it on Edgcote Lodge Hill. See Chapter 4 for a full discussion of the evidence relating to the location of the fighting.

Henry Neville the evening before. Pembroke and his brother were captured and hauled off to Northampton where they were beheaded in the presence of Warwick himself.

Despite fleeing a day earlier, Stafford prospered no better than the unfortunate Welshmen. He was seized by a West Country mob, and lynched in an act of public retribution for betraying his King.

Warwick then moved swiftly to round up Edward and his other "evil councillors". Edward himself was taken by Archbishop George Neville, which almost certainly guaranteed his life. His father-in-law, Lord Rivers, and brother-in-law Sir John Woodville were both beheaded, along with others Warwick had a score to settle with. Edward, meanwhile, was transferred to Warwick's castle in Middleham, Yorkshire.

Warwick seemed to be holding all of the cards.

What happened next does not concern us here, - suffice it to say that Warwick had seriously under estimated his opponent, and all he had done was create a path that would inexorably lead to him making common cause with Margaret of Anjou and joining the Lancastrians.

This narrative, as stated above, forms the core of the historiographical consensus of what happened in the Edgcote campaign and battle. There are problems, however.

Not all of the chronicle sources that we have agree completely with the Hall/Ramsay synthesis. Most are compatible, but where they are not they do raise questions. Ramsay did not hazard a guess at the numbers of men involved on either side, the only number he gives being the 168 Welshmen who were killed. This should come as no surprise, - Hall does not give figures for the number of men at the battle for either side, other than the 500 who made up the force of rascals.

There are also question marks as to exactly where the armies were and where they were going as they all tried to rendezvous in the East Midlands. Why, for example, were "Robin of Redesdale" and his men marching westwards towards Daventry, away from Warwick and his men approaching from London and the south east instead of towards them to effect a unification of the forces? And is it credible that Stafford and Pembroke, two men who owed their position and authority entirely to King Edward, would fall out over who should stay in an inn with a pretty maid, putting both their lives and their benefactor's Crown into jeopardy?

The whole battle narrative also requires to be tested to see what else we know, and to discuss if it is really plausible that a Welsh army could be forced to fight and be defeated in this way. And how certain are we that the fighting took place on Danes Moor, below Edgcote Lodge?

And who was "Robin of Redesdale"?

Chapter 2 - A Lack of Sources?

As discussed in the previous chapter, much of our current understanding about the battle comes from Edward Hall's work as the most complete chronicle of the campaign. Hall, however was not our only chronicler, and the frequency with which he overshadows other accounts is unfortunate.

There is a tendency with medieval battles for writers to bemoan the lack of sources. Edgcote is not immune to this complaint, - if that were not the case there would be no need for this publication. Whilst it is almost forgivable for non-military historians who write general histories of the period, it is more disappointing for those of us who study battlefields and military history.

The Battlefield Trust website, for example, says "Edgcote is one of the poorest documented of the campaigns and battles of the period", although the pages in their resource centre are some of the most detailed on the website. Similarly Philip Haigh, in his "Military Campaigns of the Wars of the Roses" says "Even by the standards of the day...actual reference to the battle is scarce"[1].

Actually the battle isn't badly served. We have nearly a dozen primary sources, in fact, provided by a selection of writers with differing backgrounds, some of whom were professional soldiers. What does make it difficult to analyse the battle is that the sources are sometimes confused in themselves, sometimes brief, and sometimes contradictory.

There are a few other very obvious things to say, that can be easily overlooked. Not all of the writings we regard as primary sources are in fact primary. Some of the most detailed are actually written by men who regarded themselves as historians of an earlier age, and make use of some of the earlier writings to provide their narrative.

Some of them, as well, provide information that could be regarded as conflicting or incompatible. What we do not know for certain is who had access to what works when writing their own account of the campaign and battle, so it isn't always easy to distinguish between corroboration and copying. (In some cases it is quite easy, - Grafton's Chronicle written in the 1560s, for example, is lifted virtually word for word from Edward Hall's Chronicle, and the writer also had a disagreement with John Stow, a contemporary historian, who accused him of copying his work as well.)

What is evident is that the narrative of the Battle of Edgcote evolved over time, before it reached its final "chronicler" form in the works of Edward Hall. However, although it evolved, not all the elements identified in the early days were carried forward to the story as we now understand it.

We have available to us, in addition to the official Royal records that tell us where Edward IV was and what he was doing, two administrative records from the Corporation of Beverley, in Yorkshire, and the Mayor of Coventry (the "Coventry

---

[1] Haigh "Military Campaigns" p100. Of course, this did not stop Haigh publishing a book on the battle two years later.

Leet Book"). Both of these give us some information about the movements of men raised and sent to fight against the rebels. As these records contain details of monies raised and spent they are probably unimpeachable as historical sources, but contain no information about the actual battle itself. For that we must rely on the poets and chroniclers.

The earliest records relating to the battle come from the works of the Welsh professional poets. The poet Guto'r Glyn (1412 – 1493) wrote a praise poem for William Herbert before he went off to battle, and then composed an elegy for him to be recited at his funeral after his execution. Guto'r Glyn was not only a poet but a professional soldier who fought in the Hundred Years' War and also for the Yorkists during the Wars of the Roses[2]. Because of the terrible Welsh losses the writing of elegies must have become a rich source of work for the wandering poets, and we also have, for example, an elegy composed for Thomas ab Roger written by Lewis Glyn Cothi (1420 -1490). These are the two best known of the Welsh poets. We have poems that celebrate the lives of the fallen from another six poets[3] although there is no readily available English translation of their works and those of Lewis Glyn Cothi, a problem for anyone who wishes to use them as a source.

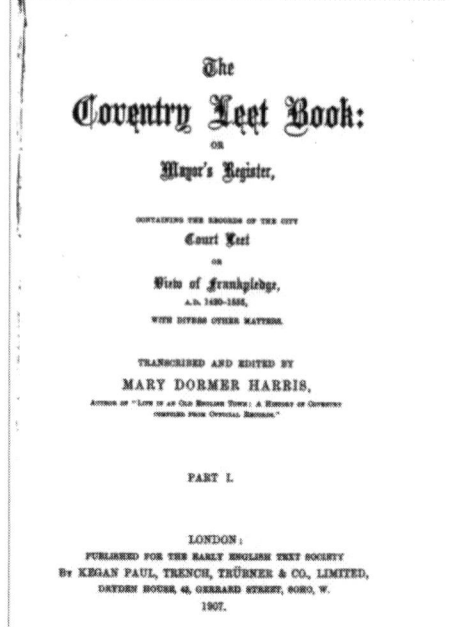

None of these poems provide a full and detailed narrative, but they do give us some important information. Lewis Glyn Cothi tells us that the forces of William Herbert were well harnessed (i.e. well supplied with armour and weapons) and therefore not what we would consider to be a typical Welsh army.

Guto'r Glyn does give a form of the narrative. He tells us that the army that Pembroke fought against was made up of Northerners from Doncaster, and that the battle was fought at Banbury. He also makes it known that the result of the battle was determined by the treachery of the Earl of Devon who fled before the Herbert brothers were both killed. What is important here is that the poems were written in Welsh, and almost certainly had no influence on the later narrative that developed amongst the writers in England, whether in the vernacular or in Latin.

---

[2] This didn't prevent him from writing a poem in praise of the Welshman who killed Richard III at Bosworth.
[3] B Lewis JMMH IX p102.

Amongst English chroniclers the earliest reference to the battle is contained in the "Itineraries" of William Worcestre (d1482). The "Itineraries" contain Worcestre's notes compiled as he journeyed around England. As they are the jottings of whatever took his fancy they are not a coherent history, and the main value is in the list of casualties for the battle that he compiled[4].

Our first account written by an English Chronicler is anonymous, and goes under the name of "A Brief Latin Chronicle", or "The concluding portion of a work entitled "Compilatio de gestis Britonum et Anglorum" ". As the text finishes abruptly in 1471, it is believed to have been prepared contemporaneously with the events discussed in its pages[5]. Written in Latin as an account of events it is brief, but it does mention Robin of Redesdale and Robin of Holderness and gives an idea of their grievances. It refers to Edward's slow response to the crisis in the North, before going on to give the date but not the location of the battle, before rounding off with an account of the Herberts' execution in Northampton (which the chronicler concludes by saying "hanc tandem justi Dei judicio pro suis sceleribus et nequiciis recepit mercedem" or the medieval equivalent of "they had it coming").

The next record in chronological sequence is that written by Jean de Wavrin (1398 – 1474), in his "Account of the chronicles and old histories of Great Britain", which takes English history up to 1471. De Wavrin was well connected and is known to have spoken to Warwick, and also presented Edward IV with a copy of the finished work. The book was written in Flemish French, and a full modern English translation is not available.

In addition to being a chronicler Jean de Wavrin was a Burgundian soldier, so not only was he writing almost contemporaneously with the battle, he was also a man who understood the subject matter. In de Wavrin's works we are told that the rebels came from the North, and were led by "le comte Wilbie" (Lord Willoughby), "accompanied by a villain called Robin of Rissedale".

In de Wavrin's narrative both Pembroke and Stafford were present at the battle. There is no mention of a deficiency of archers, and the battle takes place across a watercourse in several phases, with the rebels being saved by the arrival of timely reinforcements, before the battle finally turned when Stafford fled upon hearing of the coming of more rebel reinforcements led by Clarence. Both the Herbert brothers were then captured.

Our first English account to place the battle explicitly near Banbury is John Warkworth's Chronicle, and although it is by no means certain that it was written by Warkworth himself it was written whilst he was at Peterhouse College, Cambridge. The account dates from about 1483, and covers the first 13 years of Edward's reign. It is important to note at this point that the account was written nearly 15 years after the battle itself, so it is not an exactly contemporary account of what happened, although clearly some of those involved would still have been alive at the time should

---
[4] This list is given in the appendix to Chapter 7.
[5] "Three Fifteenth Century Chronicles" p xxi.

Warkworth have wished to speak to them or had previously done so. In modern parlance, however, we are moving from journalism to history in terms of how to look at the work.

The key facts that emerge in this account start with the rebels being raised by Robin of Redesdale in the North of England. The forces sent against them are led by Pembroke and Stafford. All of this is in the narrative that we already have from earlier writers. The chronicle then starts to add new elements. Crucially these state that Stafford's force consisted of archers (although he does not say that Pembroke does *not* have any). He goes on to say that the leaders have a disagreement in Banbury - "felle in a varyaunce for ther logynge" - and that therefore Stafford leaves before the start of the battle. He also informs us that the Herbert brothers were beheaded at Northampton. What does appear to be the case is that Warkworth does not draw upon any previous writings. The work was included in the early 16th century Antiquarian John Leland's "Collectanea", but he, Leland, is not quoted as a source by later chroniclers[6] and neither is Warkworth, until its publication by the Camden Society in 1839[7].

The Croyland Chronicle was written in Croyland or Crowland Abbey in Lincolnshire just across the north Northamptonshire border. The extract relating to the late fifteenth century period is normally known as the "Croyland Continuation", as it continues an earlier chronicle purporting to be of great antiquity. There are at least two writers, who are known as the "Second Continuator" and the "Third Continuator" respectively. They both cover the same period in differing levels of detail. The Third Continuator was well connected to Edward IV's court[8], but alas he provides us with the least detail in respect of the circumstances leading up to the battle and the battle itself. The sections relating to the Redesdale rising were written around 1486, although the Second Continuator could have been writing earlier.

Neither Croyland Continuator adds any extra details to the story, although the Second Continuator does confirm the beheadings at Northampton. Interestingly, for a man who was well connected, he does not mention Stafford at all and hence does not include the story about the lodgings.

"Hearne's Fragment", which we should note was discovered by the 18th century historian of that name, and not written by a chronicler called Hearne, is much more than a fragment as far as the Edgcote campaign is concerned. Written by a member of the Howard household, sometime between 1500 and 1522[9], the whole chronicle covers the first 13 years of Edward IV's reign, and is generally regarded as pro-Yorkist. Here we are back with the narrative as we understand it; Pembroke has no archers, Stafford and he fall out over lodgings, and Stafford retires "ten or twelve miles" following the argument. After all this clarification (including that the battle was fought at Hedgecote

---

[6] For example, Hall, to be discussed later, gives an extensive list of the works he consulted before writing his Chronicle, and neither this work nor Leland are included.
[7] Warkworth's Chronicle, Camden Society edition page ix.
[8] Ingulph's Chronicle of the Abbey of Croyland trans Riley page vii.
[9] Chronicles of the White Rose Bohn edition page v.

"on the grounds of a gentleman named Clarell"), this account introduces John Clapham to us as the leader of the rebel reinforcements whose arrival is the turning point of the battle. It is interesting to note that, although it is remarked that Pembroke has no archers, the account does not say that Stafford does, nor does it say that their absence or otherwise was crucial in determining the outcome of the battle. The Fragment also gives a name to the rebel leader, other than the pseudonym "Robin", and says it is Lord Latimer.

Our first historian that we know for certain was consulted by others and operated in close to an official capacity was Polydore Vergil (1470 – 1555). Vergil was born an Italian and became a naturalised Englishman. During his life he was a priest and diplomat as well as being an historian. His "Historia Anglia" was compiled at the request of Henry VIII around 1512-13.

Polydore Vergil's account is confused, but provides us with the first mention of there being several combats ahead of the main battle "near a village called Banbury". In this telling of the tale the battle is fought between a "Yorkshire rabble" and Pembroke. Stafford appears nowhere in the story and the reinforcements sent by Warwick are led by George, Duke of Clarence, in agreement with de Wavrin's account. What he does do is to confirm that the important beheadings occur two days after the battle.

Edward Hall (1497 – 1547) wrote his Chronicle sometime after 1530, and it has been published in several editions. The most commonly used text is from the 1809 reprinting, and that is the basis for the extract in the Sources Appendix at the end of this book.

As discussed in Chapter 1 it has a wealth of information which does not need to be repeated here. However, it is worthwhile to be reminded that most of what we consider to be the accepted narrative comes from this Chronicle. It is in the pages of Hall we first encounter the "Banbury Barmaid" who adds colour to most modern re-tellings. He also gives us lots of information on the location of the battle and the importance of the lack of archers in Pembroke's army. He is also the first writer to tell us what sources he uses, - and these include Polydore Vergil. Alas there is no indication of where the rest of his information comes from for the Redesdale Rebellion.

The last account of real note before the modern era is by John Stow (1525 – 1605). His "Annales, or a Generale Chronicle of England from Brute until the present yeare of Christ 1580" (subsequently updated to 1603) was originally published in 1580. Stow gives us less detail than Hall, but he does give us different numbers for the combatants[10]. He offers us an identity for Robin of Redesdale (Robin Hilliard) and names Sir John Conyers as one of the leaders of the rebels. He also gives us the first mention of the site of the battle being on Danesmoor, or Danes Moor. In terms of whether he is corroborating evidence for earlier writers or just repeating, we know from his own text that he read Hall's work, and was happy to quote him ("5000. (saith

---

[10] A full discussion of the size of the armies, including the figures in all of the Chroniclers' works is contained in Chapter 3.

Hall) of the Welchmen slain"). There is also a good reason to think that he had access to Warkworth's chronicle as well, - his battlefield casualty list is virtually identical using similar spelling and words.

Shortly after Stow published his book John Speed's maps of England became available. They contain a location for the battle in the map of Northamptonshire, and also give a short account of the battle, drawn from Stow.

The last full source we have is the "Herbertorum Prosapia" a family history of the Herberts, written in the 17th century. This is held in manuscript copy in the National Library of Wales, and has never been published in the modern era. It was an important source for D H Thomas' "The Herberts of Raglan and the Battle of Edgcote", and from what we can tell it drew heavily upon previously published works[11].

What this short review shows is that the narrative of the battle has evolved over time. There is a distinctly "English" narrative that encompasses Warkworth, the Croyland Continuators, the writer of Hearne's fragment, Polydore Vergil, Hall and Stow. We can prove in places that some of the works were written using others, or that the educated men who wrote them knew one another and shared their understanding of what had happened. It is not far from Croyland to Cambridge where the Warkworth Chronicle was written. By the time we get to Vergil, Hall and Stow we are certainly in the period of men who were trying to write a history of the past, not record the world around them, so we must be wary when considering them to be primary sources.

Hall was writing nearly sixty years after the battle, and Stow after the centenary. As said above, it becomes hard sometimes to tell what is corroboration and what is copying, or as Professor Anne Curry puts it when writing about another 15th century battle "Where their narratives are close or identical, this is not necessarily confirmation of veracity but of copying and interdependence"[12]. Where sources are not cited we do not know if there is a written record lost to us, or if the chroniclers are noting down folk tales and oral history. If it is the latter we should not forget that by the time many were writing Edward IV, Warwick, Clarence, Pembroke, Stafford and anyone who could claim to be Robin of Redesdale were dead and cold. Surviving the late 15th century was no easy matter.

Apart from this narrative we appear to have two independent strands. That is writers who wrote independently of each other and have a narrative that stands aside from and does not influence the English Narrative, - these are the works of the Welsh poets, and of Jean de Wavrin, which, coincidentally, are also the most contemporary accounts.

When determining what actually happened in the campaign all of the narrative threads must be considered and none favoured over any other just because it appears, metaphorically, to shout the loudest.

---

[11] Unlike most of the other sources this has not been printed in a publicly available edition nor is there a full English translation, and so it is not included in the Sources Appendix.
[12] Curry, p14.

Chapter 3 - The Numbers Game

How big were the armies that fought at the Battle of Edgcote? One of the frustrating issues when trying to understand or describe a medieval battle, and not just with Edgcote, is knowing how many people were involved. Numbers are given by chroniclers, but we have no way of knowing where the numbers come from nor their sources for stating them.

This issue is compounded in civil wars such as those that took place in late 15th century England. Although the Wars of the Roses lasted from 1455 to 1485 (or 1487 if you prefer) the periods of fighting were often short and intense with little preparation. The 1460 campaign culminating in the Battle of Northampton lasted only 14 days, ending on the 10th July. The Edgcote campaign lasted a similar length of time once the major participants became involved. There was no careful build-up such as an invasion of France, with lists of men compiled by Royal Officials nor are there store requisitions to look at. These campaigns were conducted by noblemen and their affinities. There are no payroll lists, no requests for replacement bow staves to be supplied by the Royal Armouries.

Unfortunately it has been the case for Edgcote that most historians have either side stepped this issue completely by either not giving numbers or stating that the armies were "substantial" or "considerable". Otherwise there's a tendency to pick a chronicler and go with his numbers or take a guess. Of the Victorian historians Ramsay simply doesn't give figures at all[1], whilst Oman gives 14,000 "Welsh pikemen" and 6,000 archers with Stafford[2]. He gives no number for the rebels, except to say that Pembroke's army was "greatly inferior in numbers"[3]. What does that mean? Did the rebel army number 20,000 men or more?

In the 20th century and after there's a mixed picture as well. Edgcote doesn't always feature extensively in histories of the Wars of the Roses, other than to report on the consequences of Robin of Redesdale's victory. One account deals with the battle in 24 words.[4] Philip Haigh in his book on the battle "Where both the hosts fought" states that he considers 20,000 a side to be a realistic number, although he concedes that this might be "somewhat inflated"[5]. More recently Hugh Bicheno in "Blood Royal" plumps for 6-7,000[6]. The most recent comprehensive survey of battles in this period is contained in Richard Brooks' 2005 compendium of battlefields in Britain & Ireland[7]. In the 20 battles from 1st St Albans to Stoke Field, Brooks, working on a consistent basis, provides numbers for both sides for 15 battles, and for at least one side in a

---
[1] Ramsay p338-342.
[2] Oman p185. Oman also states there were 15,000 men with Edward.
[3] Oman p187.
[4] J.R Lander "The Wars of the Roses" p126.
[5] Haigh "Where both the hosts" p117.
[6] Bicheno "Blood Royal" p125.
[7] R Brooks p228-273.

further three. In only two battles does he give up and not provide any numbers at all, - Edgcote and Losecote.

The sources we do have provide tantalising glimpses of what happened when the various sides tried to raise their forces. We know, for example, that Edward IV ordered up 1,000 sets of livery[8], and appointed someone to work on the Royal artillery train as well as crossbows, bow-staves and strings, bolts, arrows, hammers "and other necessaries" and horses[9]. We also know that he sent requests for additional troops to be provided for the suppression of the Northern rebels from towns and cities. The request to Coventry for 100 archers can be found in the Coventry Leet Book, although the city fathers only actually managed to raise 82 in total.

Although we have no administrative records for numbers of troops involved for the campaigns in the Wars of the Roses we do have an idea of the military strength of England in the mid to late 15th century. England sent armies to France on a regular basis, and we do have official records for these. For example, six years after the Battle of Edgcote Edward IV raised an army to invade France. In a united Kingdom, with all of the nobility acknowledging Edward as King, fighting against the nation's hereditary enemy, under the personal leadership of the monarch, the invasion force mustered c10,000 "archers" and c1,300 nobility and associated hangers on[10]. This was an army raised with the support of Parliament and fully funded. Modern historians, such as Anne Curry, give Henry V 13,000 men when he started the 1415 campaign[11] and about 9,000 men at Agincourt[12]. Again this was a complete English army, led by the King, although it is in popular thought considered to be small the number of men Henry V started out with was a considerable sized army by the standards of the time.

The comparison, however is not ideal. The army had to be transported to France, so the available shipping capacity would have had a limiting effect, even with the King's ability to requisition ships. Also, these armies were being raised for a longer period and required professional soldiers, - men who were prepared to leave their homes for a considerable period of time. No king would strip his realm of working age men leaving it open to invasion from Scotland, or denude the countryside of the manpower needed to plant and harvest crops. This is less of a problem if men are not going very far and for not very long.

Most campaigns in the Wars of the Roses are short. As noted above the Battle of Northampton campaign in 1460 lasts about a fortnight. The campaign that starts with Wakefield and ends at Towton is unusual, as it takes about three months. Barnet, from Edward's landing in the north to the final battle is an exact calendar month, and Tewkesbury about three weeks. Men raised for these campaigns came from several

---

[8] Warrants for Issues 9 Edw IV 18 June. Quoted in Scofield, p491.
[9] CPR 1467-1477 p163, entry for 20 June 1469.
[10] For full details on this expedition see F P Barnard's "Edward IV's French Expedition of 1475". A useful summary is given in Bicheno, p365
[11] Curry p76 - 77
[12] Curry p228

sources. Kings used Commissions of Array to raise men for war and Edward issued one in order to quell the Northern rebellions before he knew of Warwick's involvement. This empowered Warwick, amongst others, to raise and lead forces legitimately. Warwick used this authority ingeniously, it appears, as can be seen in the letter from Warwick to the Mayor of Coventry contained in the Coventry Leet Book, where Warwick asks him to ready the men of Coventry to accompany him and Clarence to the North to meet up with the King. These were men Edward had already instructed Coventry to raise.

Secondly, noblemen and large magnates would call for members of their affinity to join them as repayment for their "good lordship" in a form of feudal relationship. There may have been an element of compulsion in such assemblies of men, or at least an implicit threat that if a man did not follow his immediate master when asked he might find himself in difficult personal circumstances afterwards. Armies might also be joined by those looking for some form of recompense through loot gained. As Polydore Vergil put it: " The Yorkeshyremen, well satisfyed with this fortunate fyght, waxed soodaynly more coole, and therefor procedyd no further forward, but loden with pay[13] drew homeward". Affinities could vary enormously in size depending on the power and influence of the noble concerned. Warwick, for example, could raise considerably more men from his holdings than Lords Berkeley and Lisle did when they settled a personal dispute at Nibley Green in March 1470.

Finally, of course, depending on who was backing who, either or both armies might include foreign troops or mercenaries. Edward IV had Burgundians at Towton[14], and the presence of French mercenaries at Bosworth and landsknechts at Stoke Field are well attested, not to mention the use of Scottish and Irish mercenaries as well.

But do we have an idea of what sized armies could be expected to be raised to undertake a civil war within England at a time when the population is estimated to be about 2 million?[15] This number is down from the pre-Black Death highs of the 14th century when the population was more than double the size it would be in late 15th century England. Handed down memory may think in terms of armies being much bigger than they could be in a country that was much more sparsely populated.

It is important to take a moment to consider the numbers we are going to discuss. At the start of the 15th century the population of London was probably no bigger than 30,000, and that of York less than 10,000[16]. Whilst in the post industrial revolution period we are used to seeing large crowds of 40,000 or more at football games or demonstrations, medieval man or woman would very rarely have seen a collection of people together that big. That may mean that when trying to estimate how many people

---

[13] This is usually read as meaning "loot", not a formal issue of pay as we would understand it
[14] Haigh "Military Campaigns" p58
[15] This number is taken from the Wikipedia entry "Demography of England". Whilst I would normally baulk at quoting Wikipedia as a reference, the sources used for the article look to be reputable
[16] Pop 7,248 in 1377, taken from Wikipedia entry quoting W. G. Hoskins (1984). "Local History in England", based on Poll Tax records.

are in a large group our medieval ancestors may have lacked appropriate reference points.

We may have one clue as to how big armies were expected to be, in an Act passed by Henry VI's parliament in 1453[17]. Under the Act, Parliament granted the King 20,000 archers. Of these 1,000 were remitted on Royal favour, 3,000 were to be provided by the Lords, 3,000 by Wales and Chester and the balance by Counties and Cities[18]. The men were granted with several restrictions, however. They were only to serve for 6 months, they were not to serve overseas, and the providers were to be given 4 months notice.

This grant was given the year following Richard of York's aborted attempt to force his way into the King's favour that came to an end at Crayford Heath near Dartford in March 1452. It would therefore seem to be a force intended for the quelling of internal dissension, or possibly a foreign invasion. Given the length of time to call it out, and the likely length of any campaign, it appears to be more of a deterrent in waiting, a statement of loyal support or a proxy for the raising of taxes than a practical means to fight a war.

However, what it does indicate is the size of an army that Henry VI, his advisers and Parliament thought it practical to raise and also suitable to its purpose. It would imply, therefore, that this is about as big a force of archers as anyone was likely to need. In effect it provides a cap on any numbers when considering who might be called out. Although, perhaps, we should take into account the records from Coventry which show that an attempt to raise 100 men ended up falling short by about 20% (perhaps in practice the request for 100 was too many, - Parliament rated them at 76 for the purposes of the Act).

The final point to be noted here is that it is important to consider exactly who was involved in the actual battle and also, just as importantly, who was not. The Edgcote campaign does not sit comfortably under the heading of being part of The Wars of the Roses. As stated in the introduction, you will look in vain for anyone sporting the Red Rose of Lancashire, either literally or figuratively. The major Lancastrian nobles were not actively involved in the campaign. Margaret of Anjou was in France with Prince Edward, and Henry VI was in the Tower of London. In fact, the number of Earls, Dukes, Barons and other nobles who might be regarded as Yorkists not involved is considerable. Perhaps what we are seeing as well is the collective ruling class of England drawing breath to see whether the protégé or the old master is to prevail.

In continuing this point, not only were significant nobles and their affinities not involved, even those involved in the campaign were not all present at the battle. Warwick and Clarence were not present and neither were Edward IV and Lord Hastings, the latter being one of the King's principal supporters and beneficiary of Edward's largesse.

---

[17] Ramsay p161
[18] Full list quoted in Ramsay p175

All of this points towards forces present at the battle which might be smaller than those conventionally considered to have been there.

With this as background we can turn to look at the numbers contained in the chroniclers. In Chapter 2 the sources were discussed in terms of their immediacy to the battle and also how they might have influenced one another. Here we can look at what they actually say about the number of combatants present and weigh how reliable they might be.

Not all of the sources give numbers. Our earliest sources, the poems written by the Welsh Bards, are long on atmosphere but are short on hard numbers for the men present during the campaign. And of the sources that do give numbers, not all of them give numbers for all the forces involved.

Let us start with the rebel army, led by Robin of Redesdale. The Welsh poets, Jean de Wavrin, William of Worcester, the "Brief Latin Chronicle" and John Warkworth all fail to give us numbers for the rebel army. The earliest source with a number for the army is the Second Continuator of the Croyland Chronicle. This gives the incredible number of 60,000 men who set out from the North to march to London to join Warwick. The number presents several problems, as all of the published versions of the Chronicle are in English, whereas the original would have been in Latin and the numbers given in roman numerals. There are several ways this could have been written, - sixty lots of M, for example, or LX written with lines over the top, signifying thousands, or, as seen in other sources "LX. M". Whilst the X and M would probably be indisputable, it is conceivable that it originally read as "IX", or 9,000, and the higher number is due to a copying error or a simple misreading of a monk's handwriting. Whatever is the case, 60,000 would certainly be a very large army, even by the standards of later centuries when armies were drawing men from a significantly larger population, and the casual way that the Chronicler refers to the number without commenting on the size of the army would point towards an interpretation with the lower of the two numbers.

The next source chronologically, known as "Hearne's Fragment", refers to the Northern men fighting at "Hedgecote" and again refuses to enlighten us about the rebel strength. Thereafter, our chroniclers are not so reticent.

We then come to Polydore Vergil. He gives a number for the rebels gathered at York written as "xv^{ten} thousand", which is usually taken to mean 15,000, but otherwise his details of the campaign are weak.

Polydore Vergil is followed by Hall's Chronicle. This, as discussed in Chapter 2, is the fullest of sources, and he does not disappoint. Although he does not give us a number at the battle he does state that the rebellion started in York with 15,000 men (written as "xv thousand"). Unfortunately for us, Hall also makes clear in the introduction to his book that one of the authorities he consulted was Polydore Vergil, so this looks more like repetition than confirmation of a number, especially as it also places the men at York. (NB this number would have been nearly twice the population of the City, - a truly imposing figure).

After Hall we have a gap of nearly 50 years before John Stow picks up the story again. He quotes 20,000 for the rebels, although it is interesting to note that there are several editions of his "Annales". This number comes from the "Annales to 1580" edition. By the "Annales to 1603" the number is reduced to 2000. What is interesting about both of these numbers is that we know, from other evidence in the annals, that Stow used Hall as a source. However here Stow has chosen to use numbers different to those quoted in Hall. This begs the question as to what was Stow's missing reference for these numbers?

Finally we have the personal history of the Herberts, the "Herbertorum Prosapia". This quotes 20,000 rebels[19], however as we will see below, the prima facie evidence is that the Herbert's personal chronicler simply took the numbers straight out of the 1580 version of Stow's Annales.

Given all of these considerations, and **IF** we assume a transcription error in the Croyland Chronicle and a typographical error in Stow's 1603 version, the Chroniclers give us a number in the range 9,000 – 20,000 men setting out from the region of York. If this range of numbers is correct, by the time the army arrived in the Banbury area to fight Pembroke the numbers would have been reduced by men dropping out or skipping home with their loot. However, another large caveat is required here. Some of the confusion that arises in the works of the chroniclers is due to what appears to be more than one rebel movement in the North. Haigh identifies three rebellions, as does Keith Dockray[20], which start in April and run through to late June/early July, when the rebels start to head south. There is therefore about a three month gap from the incident which gives us the numbers outside the gates of York to the Battle of Edgcote, a time during which the rebels are put down twice and are forced into a change of leader(s) due to executions.

Following on from the rebels let us now review the evidence for the main force sent to confront them, that is the force from South Wales, led by William Herbert, the Earl of Pembroke. We are more fortunate than with the rebels, when looking at the earliest sources. Although the Welsh poets, Worcestre, the "Brief Latin Chronicler" and de Wavrin again give us no numbers, not so John Warkworth. Warkworth gives us a number of 43,000, although this is written in roman numerals as xliij. M. Interestingly, the Welsh historian, H T Evans, took this number to be read as 13,000.[21] Certainly, if you again consider the possibility of a copying error from the original document the number could be xiiij. M, or 14,000[22]. The Croyland Chronicle, which

---

[19] I have been unable to track down a readily available English language version of the Herbertorum Prosapia. I regret that all the numbers quoted are taken from third parties referring to or quoting from the HP.

[20] Haigh "Where both the hosts" p16 -28; K R Dockray ""The Yorkshire Rebellions of 1469"

[21] H T Evans p103

[22] This conclusion is also reached by the original compiler of Warkworth's Chronicle for the Camden Society in 1839. See note on p44. This point is overlooked by Haigh in "Where both the hosts". See p116.

caused such discussion in respect of the rebels above, merely states that he had a "considerable body of troops". What this means it is difficult to say, but given that the Chronicler has given a number for the rebels he would be unlikely to call a number much smaller than their forces "considerable". That might push an argument for an army around the size of the rebels, or even slightly larger. However, as we shall see below, the Croyland Chronicler completely omits to mention Stafford's force, so his men may be included in the "considerable" number.

Hearne's Fragment is the first to break ranks with the other chroniclers and give us a number that is unequivocally less than 10,000. The Fragment records a number of 7,000 or 8,000, and was originally written in the vernacular. The printed version uses "seven or eight thousand" so it is likely this is an accurate reproduction of the original.

Hall, as befits the man who wrote most about the battle, does have a figure for Pembroke's men and says 6-7,000 men (written as "vi or vii thousande"). This number is Hall's own, as Polydore Vergil gives no numbers for any of the other forces, except the rebels. Whatever the source was, it is ignored by Stow who confidently states that there were 18,000 "Welchmen[23]". This number is quoted again in the "Herbertorum Prosapia", reinforcing the view that the author was taking the numbers from Stow, or from Stow's source.

Taking into account the possible error in Warkworth the sources give us a force size of between 6,000 and 18,000, which is comparable to that which we determined for the rebels above.

When looking at Stafford's force we start off with an oddity, - we have a number in de Wavrin (although, again nothing in the Welsh poets nor Worcestre). De Wavrin states that when "Stamfort" (sic) fled from the battle he took 7-8,000 men with him ("sept a huit mille hommes"). This number accords closely with Warkworth, who states 7,000 (written as "vij. M archers"). The Croyland Chronicler has no number for Stafford, and in fact makes no mention of him or his men at all, not at the battle, nor before and even omits the salacious story of the commanders falling out over lodgings.

Hearne also has good numbers for Stafford's men, and places his strength at 4,000 -5,000, written without any trace or possibility of ambiguity. Polydore Vergil again doesn't trouble us with any detail or reference to Stafford, so Hall, once more, is using a different source. His number for Stafford's men is an unambiguous 800, - written clearly as "eight hundred archers". Note that Hall, or his publisher, is profligate in his choice of whether to use arabic or roman numerals or to write the numbers out in full. With one exception, also in Hall, this is the smallest number given for any force. Stow also continues to go his own way, and quotes 6,000 ("6000") in both editions. He, again, is copied by the "Herbertorum Prosapia".

We therefore have quite a range of numbers, running from 800 to 8,000 although, possibly significantly, they cluster around the upper end of 4,000 – 8,000.

---

[23] This is the same in both editions, unlike the rebel numbers.

When we come to the decisive reinforcements the chroniclers start to fall apart a bit in terms of any consensus. Several accounts (Croyland, Warkworth, Stow, Herbertorum Prosapia) do not mention the arrival of the rebel reinforcements at all. Polydore Vergil writes that the Duke of Clarence and the Earl of Warwick are present "having joygnyd ther forces marchyd to a village caulyd Banbery" and the wording could mean either that they join the Northerners before the battle or part way through. Hearne's Fragment states that Clapham is sent out from London with 15,000 men ("fifteen thousand"), whilst Hall says that Clapham arrives with only 500 men (written as "CCCCC"), and these are collected from around Northampton, not brought from London. De Wavrin doesn't give any numbers although he implies that there may have been two groups of reinforcements, the first led by two knights (named as Sir Geoffrey Gates and Sir William Parr[24]) and the rumour of a second wave led by Clarence, which may not get to the battlefield at all.

With only two numbers, and not even a hint of correlation, it seems we can say very little at all about the number of rebel reinforcements, based upon the sources. However, it might be useful to note here that people at the time, following on from remarks made above about the size of towns and populations, may well have found it easier to estimate accurately smaller numbers.

The last quantitative number we can take from the sources is that for casualties. Croyland gives the number of 4,000 for both armies, which we can expect to be disproportionately weighted towards the losing army. Although the losing army normally takes much larger casualties than the winner we do know that the fighting was hard, due to the named noble casualties on both sides, so a split of 1,000 rebels to 3,000 Royalists would be possible. Warkworth gives us 2,000 Welshmen ("two.M") slain, and no rebels. Otherwise we have more than 5,000 in Hall ("above v. M") which is quoted in Stow ("5,000 saith Hall"). Given the numbers estimated for the total army are in the range 6-18,000 this represents a massive casualty level. It is possible that the Welsh causalities were high as a proportion. They were a beaten army that had previously given no quarter and were fleeing to a natural choke point in trying to get across the River Cherwell. However it is difficult to extrapolate from the number of casualties to a full army size, other than to assume it must have been bigger than the number of people killed.

What is clear from this survey is that whilst we have numbers for the armies and components in the campaign, we don't necessarily have numbers for the armies that made it to Edgcote itself. This is an important point. As was stated above, the armies that fight are not fully assembled. Whether or not Stafford is at the battle (e.g. Hall says no, de Wavrin says yes) the Royalist army is incomplete. The King's forces, which would probably be of a similar size if not larger are not present. Similarly Warwick would have expected his main fighting strength to have come from the South, as he

---

[24] The presence of Gates and Parr is rejected by Haigh "Where both the hosts" p119. This is on the basis that he believes the account of the battle by de Wavrin refers to Tewkesbury not Edgcote (p115). De Wavrin's full text does not support this definitive conclusion. See Chapter 4 below.

marched up from Kent. So if we take the 20,000 figure from the Henry VI act of Parliament as a ballpark figure for a national turnout we must expect the armies to be smaller than that, by around half at least.

When considering the size of the battle the next port of call is to look at other battles fought in the period and see how they compare. We are fortunate that we have quite a large sample size. If we take Richard Brooks' list[25] discussed above we have 20 battles in which there are 40 armies involved and he provides numbers for 35 of them. Not only that, we also have data for which nobles were present, so comparisons and conclusions can be drawn. The data from the book is compiled in the table in the Appendix to this chapter. NB for the purposes of this exercise where Brooks has given a range of numbers I have opted for the higher of the two values.

Before we consider the data there are three observations that need to be made first. These principals apply generally to battles in this period. There are exceptions that can be identified – such as when an ambush is planned and executed – but there are three general commonalities that apply to Wars of the Roses battles:

1) Armies fight by mutual consent, because both expect to win. Having identified where the enemy is armies usually form up on suitable ground and offer battle if they are prepared to fight.
2) Because of point 1 armies are generally of comparable power, or at least they perceive themselves to be so. Differences in numbers might be made up in confident leadership or troop quality.
3) Armies generally deploy without reserves[26] as successful generals lead from the front and didn't want to be outflanked.

At first glance the table seems to be unhelpful. The numbers are all over the place, ranging from a few hundred to 20 – 25,000. However a few simple observations can help to make sense of what is going on here, in the light of what has been discussed above.

As was said at the start of this chapter the building blocks of an army start with a noble's affinity. Given that statement it would be helpful to have an idea of what sort of force a noble man could raise without resorting to extreme measures. In that respect Nibley Green is a helpful starting point. We know these numbers are fairly reliable, and we also know that there is one affinity aside. From that we can see that a man of influence without being a major magnate, such as William Lord Berkeley, can raise

---

[25] Brooks numbers are based upon Professor Ferdinand Lot's work,"*L'art militaire et les armées au Moyen Âge*", and take into account the physical size of the battlefields on which the armies deployed. All numbers used with the kind permission of Mr Brooks.
[26] This is a contentious issue, as this may not have been the case earlier, when English armies did not rely so heavily on archers and men at arms on foot. There are instances of reserves being used in the earlier medieval period, and also at some battles in the Wars of the Roses, but generally speaking this is not the case.

about 1,000 men. This is supported by the battle at Clyst Bridge where a similar observation can be made with one affinity aside.

Then look at Mortimer's Cross, with two noblemen aside, in the depths of Winter, - again, affinity sizes of approximately 1,000. You can also add Hedgeley Moor to that list. These numbers also carry across to 1st St Albans, which blows up in a hurry at a time when neither side is expecting to fight a war and preparations are lighter than happen later.

Of course not every battle and every nobleman falls into this size range. Some noblemen, the "magnates", command significantly bigger affinities and have access to more substantial resources. The most obvious of these is the Earl of Warwick, followed by the Dukes of Buckingham and the Percies. To this list, at the time of Edgcote, might be added William Herbert, Earl of Pembroke, who dominated Wales due to family possessions and the gifts from the King.

The heads of the Houses of York and Lancaster clearly could command large followings as well, and when in possession of the throne, or able to act with apparent authority, could use the instruments of the state, such as Commissions of Array, to raise large forces. Whilst it is not a hard and fast rule, the general principal is that the presence of a leader such as Edward IV or Margaret of Anjou will result in the army size being larger.

What does this tell us of Edgcote? If we start with Stafford the number of 800 for his army given in Hall looks believable for a noble marching with his immediate retainers and affinity.

Pembroke's army is certainly larger, - the chroniclers who give numbers all concur on that point. If we regard him as a Great Magnate, able to pull out three or four times more men than his less well-endowed contemporaries (or more) that would give a number with a maximum of about 4,000 men, a not inconsiderable number for a nobleman to raise on his own account. That would mean the combined army of Pembroke and Stafford might be 5,000 men. If we were to assume a fully formed army aimed to put down a rebellion with Edward present was intended to be about 7,000 to 10,000 men, - the range of army sizes that encompass Northampton, Towton, Barnet and Bosworth – then this number fits within that range as a significant component of the final army.

Robin of Redesdale's force is more problematic. We know it was instigated by Warwick, and there is evidence that he had a component of his own affinity – 300 archers - present at earlier disturbances.[27] Other Warwick retainers and followers are also in the force, - Sir Henry Neville the son of Lord Latimer, and Sir John Conyers the Younger are named as they are both killed[28]. The force might also include men

---

[27] Letter from W M Monipenny to Louis XI, quoted in de Wavrin, Dupont edition 1863 Vol 4 p193. This letter is dated 14th January 1467. Haigh "Where both the hosts" p16 erroneously dates it to 1469.

[28] See Warkworth's Chronicle, repeated almost verbatim in Stow. NB Warkworth refers to "Sir Henry Latimer". This error is corrected in Hall. See discussion in Chapter 6 about the real identity of Robin of Redesdale.

from the North with genuine grievances or on the look out for loot, so would be bigger than that which Warwick might raise from his own resources.

The main part of Warwick's army intended for this campaign was coming from Calais and Kent, picking up supporters on the way North. This army has been put at being 15,000 strong, but a more realistic number, based on what Warwick brought with him in the campaign of Northampton in 1460, is 10,000. That implies a smaller number than 10,000 for Redesdale's men, as they are coming from a less populated area, aren't pulling the full power of Warwick's affinity nationwide, and will have suffered some attrition on the march south. With Warwick's power in the North, and the presence of Lord Latimer's son, we might hazard that the army might be a minimum of 3,000, rising to at least 5,000 if they were prepared to fight Pembroke before Warwick and Clarence arrived from London. In this case we know that they were willing to fight, as they had diverted towards Banbury from Northampton, and had been in touch with Pembroke's forces for a couple of days. If they were aware of the movements of Warwick and Clarence and the location of the advance guard under Clapham, Gates and Parr they may have been prepared to engage with Pembroke in anticipation of the arrival of overwhelming force. Pembroke, on the other hand, had lost the strategic scouting battle, having been driven back from Northampton, and may have been unaware of the proximity of some of Warwick's other forces.

The final point to consider, especially in the light of the comments above about armies deploying where they are prepared to give battle, is the ground on which the armies drew up and the area in which they ended up fighting.

The most likely location for the actual battle is discussed in detail in Chapter 4, including the hill where Pembroke's army was initially deployed. The location is now identified by the presence of Edgcote Lodge Farm at the eastern end of the crest. The hill is prominent in the area, but has a fairly flat top, before it falls away quite steeply to the West, South and East. The area available for deployment is approximately 800 - 1,000 yards long. The actual depth of units in the late medieval period that aren't using pikes in the Swiss fashion is debatable, but for our purposes here it is likely that the formation depth was 4-6 men, with each man on a frontage of two feet to a yard.

Given these parameters we get the following range of numbers for the army:

Position Length	Frontage per man	Ranks Deep 4	Ranks Deep 6
800 yards	2 feet	4,800 men	7,200 men
	3 feet	3,200 men	4,800 men
1,000 yards	2 feet	6,000 men	9,000 men
	3 feet	4,000 men	6,000 men

As can be seen in order to fit in an army even approaching the upper end of the chronicler's numbers on to the battlefield, the men would have to have been close packed and formed up deep, and making use of the more difficult ground to the western end of the hill. Depending upon when Stafford took his army away, - and one source says he fled during the battle – the position would have been chosen to allow him to deploy as well. That might argue for a lower number at the actual fight, deployed on a wider frontage per man or with a less deep formation.

The rebel force's deployment area is of a similar length, although it runs more North to South, so there is no need to re-perform the calculations above. The anecdotal evidence in Hall relating to Sir Richard Herbert's feat of arms with a poleaxe implies a formation towards the narrower depth of our spectrum, and so in turn points us towards the lower numbers until the arrival of their reinforcements. The chronicles generally either suggest, or state outright, that the "Northmen" initiated or were willing participants in the fighting, so it might be argued that they would have been of equal or greater strength than Pembroke's men, but if they were in a thinner formation as implied by Sir Richard's exploits then that would argue both armies down to the lower end of the numbers, in the 3,000 - 5,000 range.

Consideration of the ground is not helpful in respect of the size of the final reinforcements that tip the balance in favour of the rebels. If Hall is to be believed, - that they amounted to only 500 men – then that might support the view that the armies were smaller rather than larger all round if such a small number was to prove decisive.

As can be seen from this survey of the evidence available to us from a range of different sources and approaches it is difficult to come to any decisive conclusion, except, perhaps that the armies were likely to be counted more in four figure numbers than five. Even to get to this point there is a not entirely healthy amount of speculation in some of the arguments used above. However, it is clear that the larger numbers favoured by some of the chroniclers and historians do not fit with what was happening in the campaign, what it was practically possible for the participants to raise and the numbers that would be able to fight on the battlefield chosen by both sides.

Appendix to "The Numbers Game"

Battle	Date		Commanders	Combatants
1st St Albans	22 May 1455	Winner	Richard, Duke of York Richard Neville, Earl of Salisbury Richard Neville, Earl of Warwick	3,000
		Loser	Henry VI Edward Beaufort, Duke of Somerset Henry Stafford, Duke of Buckingham	2,000
Clyst Bridge	15 Dec 1455	Winner	Thomas Courtney, Earl of Devon	1,000
		Loser	William Bonville	600
Blore Heath	23 Sep 1459	Winner	Richard Neville, Earl of Salisbury	5,000
		Loser	James Touchet, Lord Audley	8,000
Ludford Bridge	12 Oct 1459	Winner	Henry VI Margaret of Anjou	12,000
		Loser	Richard, Duke of York Richard Neville, Earl of Salisbury Richard Neville, Earl of Warwick	7,000
Northampton[1]	10 Jul 1460	Winner	Edward, Earl of March (future Ed IV) Richard Neville, Earl of Warwick William Neville, Lord Fauconberg	10,000
		Loser	Henry VI Humphrey Stafford, Duke of Buckingham John Talbot, Earl of Shrewsbury Thomas Percy, Lord Egremont John Beaumont, Viscount Beaumont Edmund Grey, Lord Grey of Ruthin	6,000
Wakefield	31 Dec 1460	Winner	Henry Beaufort, Duke of Somerset Henry Percy, Earl of Northumberland Lord John Clifford	15,000
		Loser	Richard, Duke of York Richard Neville, Earl of Salisbury	6,000
Mortimer's Cross	3 Feb 1461	Winner	Edward, Earl of March William Herbert	2,000
		Loser	Jasper Tudor, Earl of Pembroke James Butler, Earl of Wiltshire	3,000
2nd St Albans	17 Feb 1461	Winner	Margaret of Anjou Lord John Clifford Henry Percy, Earl of Northumberland Henry Beaufort, Duke of Somerset Henry Holland, Duke of Exeter John Talbot, Earl of Shrewsbury	20,000
		Loser	Richard Neville, Earl of Warwick William Neville, Lord Fauconberg John Mowbray, Duke of Norfolk John de la Pole, Duke of Suffolk	25,000

[1] These numbers differ from Brooks, and are based on the work of the Northamptonshire historian, Mike Ingram.

Battle	Date		Commanders	Combatants
Towton[2]	29 Mar 1461	Winner	Edward IV Richard Neville, Earl of Warwick William Neville, Lord Fauconberg John Mowbray, Duke of Norfolk	7,000
		Loser	Henry Percy, Earl of Northumberland Henry Beaufort, Duke of Somerset	7,000
Hedgeley Moor	25 Apr 1464	Winner	John Neville, Marquess of Montagu	Unknown
		Loser	Henry Beaufort, Duke of Somerset Ralph Percy	1,500
Hexham	15 May 1464	Winner	John Neville, Marquess of Montagu	4,000
		Loser	Henry Beaufort, Duke of Somerset	500
Nibley Green	20 Mar 1470	Winner	Lord William Berkeley	1,000
		Loser	Thomas Talbot, Viscount Lisle	300
Barnet	14 Apr 1471	Winner	Edward IV Richard, Duke of Gloucester William, Lord Hastings	10,000
		Loser	Richard Neville, Earl of Warwick John Neville, Marquess of Montagu John de Vere, Earl of Oxford Henry Holland, Duke of Exeter	13,000
Tewkesbury	4 May 1471	Winner	Edward IV Richard, Duke of Gloucester William, Lord Hastings	5,000
		Loser	Margaret of Anjou Edmund Beaufort, Duke of Somerset	6,000
Bosworth	22 Aug 1485	Winner	Henry Tudor John de Vere, Earl of Oxford Sir William Stanley	8,000
		Loser	Richard III John Howard, Duke of Norfolk Henry Percy, Earl of Northumberland	7,900
Tadcaster	10 Jun 1487	Winner	John de la Pole, Earl of Lincoln	Unknown
		Loser	Lord Henry Clifford	400
Stoke Field	16 Jun 1487	Winner	Henry VII John de Vere, Earl of Oxford	12,000
		Loser	John de la Pole, Earl of Lincoln	8,000
Blackheath	17 Jun 1497	Winner	Henry VII Lord Daubeney	25,000
		Loser	J Touchet, Lord Audley	15,000

---

[2] In an email exchange with Richard Brooks he revised his estimates down from c20,000 a side. This is consistent with Ramsay, p278 who says a number of c5,000 would cover the position.

Chapter 4 - Location, Location, Location

In understanding any battle the first and often most important piece of evidence we have is the ground it was fought on. Commanders quite often choose ground deliberately, and for a number of reasons. The chosen area has to be big enough to deploy their army, and hopefully it must give it some advantage, - but not necessarily so much advantage that an opponent refuses to fight. Unless, of course, it is the intention to avoid conflict. Medieval battles, for all their bloodshed and violence, do not often leave a mark upon the landscape. If we are lucky we may find arrow heads or cannon balls or the odd buckle. Sometimes we may find cast off weapons or grave pits. However generally the battles are very ecologically friendly. Weapons and armour left on the battlefield will not have remained there long as iron and steel was a valuable resource. Clothing would have been stripped from corpses, and the hafts of spears and pole axes will at the very least make fire wood. Often the only artefact we have left is the very ground itself, so determining what ground the battle was fought on is of great importance.

We are fortunate in many ways that we have quite a bit of information about where the Battle of Edgcote was fought. Where we are less fortunate is that not all of the evidence our chroniclers have given us fits together in a clean and helpful fashion.

What we do have is sufficiently intriguing and ambiguous that modern historians from Oman and Ramsay through to Haigh and Bicheno have been able to develop their own theories, supported by maps showing the precise positioning of the various armies and their movements both prior to and during the battle. It is the intention of this chapter to look at the evidence as to where the armies fought, and what manoeuvres were followed, and hopefully draw a sustainable conclusion. However, it is also the case that we must accept that we cannot necessarily be as certain as we might like to be.

To start on a positive note at least initially we have a very good and consistent record of the general area that the battle was fought in across all of the sources. There is very little doubt that the battle was fought near Banbury. Our earliest source, Guto'r Glyn, refers to "the evil of Banbury[1]". His contemporary Lewys Glyn Cothi gives us the following couplet:

Ban fu fatel ein gelyn ym Manbri oer ym mhen bryn	When our enemy's army was on a hilltop at wretched Banbury,

H T Evans' classic book "Wales and the Wars of the Roses" even refers to it as "The Battle of Banbury"[2].

---
[1] "drwg Banberi".
[2] H T Evans p105.

There is some dispute in respect of one of our early sources. De Wavrin's work has been rejected by some writers as he refers to the battle being near "Theosbury". This has been taken by some historians, notably Haigh, to refer to the Battle of Tewkesbury[3]. However, it is more likely that de Wavrin had misheard an English name or made an error in his notes about a "-bury" named town. He states specifically that the town of "Theosbury" is 80 miles from London ("de la Londres environs quatre vingtz milles"). This distance is most likely given in Roman miles of 5,000 feet, instead of a modern mile of 5,280 feet, so in modern terms this would be just under 76 miles.

Although we don't know de Wavrin's starting point for this measurement, the distance from Charing Cross in London to Banbury on foot by today's roads, avoiding motorways, is about 73 miles. The distance to Tewkesbury, starting from the same point is over 100 miles[4] or slightly more than 105 Roman miles. De Wavrin may have got the place name wrong, but he doesn't seem to have been wrong about the location. The only other place name in his account is Northampton, which would seem to confirm that he is writing about the East Midlands not the South West, so de Wavrin adds to the body of evidence pointing towards Banbury, at the very least, if not Edgcote. De Wavrin also provides topographical references not found elsewhere, which we will return to later.

Other early references are equally brief or briefer. Our most contemporary reference is in the Coventry Leet Book, that tells us that Lord Herbert was taken in a battle by Banbury. William Worcestre in his "Itineraries" helpfully gives us a clear reference to "Edgcote Field near Banbury"[5]. Warkworth merely gives us "a playne byyonde Banbury toune". The Croyland Continuator provides further confirmation stating the armies met "on the plain of Hegge-cote[6], near Banbury, in the county of Northampton". These latter two references are useful, as they confirm that the fighting took place on a piece of low lying flat ground, or a "plain".

Our anonymous "Brief Latin Chronicle" writer gives no detail, other than to imply that the battle was near Northampton.

Although a reference to Edgcote cuts down the area beyond Banbury where the battle might be fought, it should be noted that the area which can be described as being Edgcote or near Edgcote is a rectangle about 1½ miles by 2½ miles, with its corners at Chipping Warden, Culworth, Thorpe Mandeville and Wardington[7], starting in the North Western corner, and moving round clockwise. This is actually quite a large area for an English medieval battlefield, and we need to refine the location considerably to determine the exact location for the fighting.

---

[3] Haigh "Where both the hosts" p115. The Saxon name for Tewkesbury was "Theocsbury".
[4] Distance calculated using Google Maps.
[5] Haigh "Where both the hosts" p118. This is an English translation of the Latin text. I do not know how "Edgcote" was spelled in the original.
[6] Referred to as "Hegecot" in the third continuation.
[7] Ordnance Survey Explorer Series Map 206.

Our first clue as to where, exactly, it might be (together with one of our many different spellings of Edgcote), is given in Hearne's Fragment, which says the armies "drew nigh to Banbury to a place called Hedgecote upon the grounds of a gentleman named Clarell". The intriguing reference to lands belonging to Clarell leaves us wanting to know what lands Clarell owned in order to narrow the area down a bit.

Richard Clarell, it turns out, was a bit of a local magnate, and either owned or farmed the Manor of "Ochecote" in the late 15th century, as well as having permission to farm neighbouring land as well. If the lands of Edgcote Manor were the same in the late 15th century as they were in the 18th century, from when we have an estate map, his lands were bordered on the north by the River Cherwell, and on the east by a tributary to the same river. In the other directions there are no clear natural boundaries, but we can see that these were approximately the lines that coincide with modern landmarks. These are to the south by the line of the now disused railway and to the west by the long distance footpath known as the Jurassic Way.

A court case in 1499 brought against his widow, Margaret, and several other co-defendants by the Bishop of Lincoln identifies some land held by his beneficiaries as being "600 acres of land, 60 acres of meadow, 600 acres of pasture, 100 acres of wood and 100 shillings of rent"[8]. As part of the land is meadow that might indicate that he owned or farmed land on a flood plain, or near water. However note that this refers to some, not all, of Richard Clarell's land, and might not be the part of his estate where the battle was fought and so does not determine exactly where the fighting might have taken place. It does, however, add "Ochecote" to the number of different spellings we have for Edgcote.

Moving on to the reign of Henry VIII, Polydore Vergil's account gives us "a village called Banbury", which seems to be a step backwards in terms of refining the location, but that is not unusual for his account of this campaign and battle, which is muddled, brief and vague. Fortunately for us Edward Hall does not disappoint, and confirms "in a faire plain, nere to a toune called Hedgecot, three myle from Banbery". Hall also provides further details that apparently fix the battle in its exact location which will be discussed below. This is fortunate, as Edgcote is actually closer to six miles from Banbury than three (measured from Banbury Cross to Edgcote village), and so relying on the distance given by Hall would place the battle outside the rectangle given above, and in the Lordship of Wardington, not the Manor of Edgcote.

John Stow's Annales, although he used Hall as a source, gives us a further place name reference to refine where within our rectangle the battle was fought. He says, quite clearly, "a plaine called Danes more, néere to ye towne of Edgecote, iij. miles frō Babery". It can be seen that Stow is practically repeating verbatim Hall's location, but with the addition of the detail that the name of the plain was "Danes Moor".

---

[8] http://www.medievalgenealogy.org.uk/fines/abstracts/CP_25_1_179_98.shtml item 58. I owe this reference to Mike Ingram.

The site of the battle on Danes Moor is marked very clearly on John Speed's county map of 1603[9] with the symbol of a tent. A box to the side of the map states "At Edgcote in this county upon Danes Moor a bloody battle was fought".

Danes Moor is identified on modern Ordnance Survey maps[10], and the name was believed by Baker, the 19th century Northamptonshire County historian, to date from at least 1469[11], based upon the work of John Morton, the early 18th century naturalist, and clergyman in Great Oxenden. The reference to the Danes allegedly refers to a battle between the Danes and Saxons in 914AD.

It would probably be good to stop and draw breath at this point and note that the name of the battle has either been the Battle of Banbury (preferred by Welsh sources and writers) or the Battle of Edgcote/Heggecote/Hegecote, or perhaps the Battle of Danes Moor. It was never called "The Battle of Edgcote Moor", as it appears in some on-line resources, as Edgcote Moor is not actually a place. The only named Moor in the area is Danes Moor.

Before we go on to look in more detail at the other clues we have from the sources and the theories of modern writers it is important to bear in mind that the landscape has changed since the time of the battle. It has already been noted that a disused railway line runs along the southern edge of the area in question, which makes use of both cuttings and embankments[12]. Elsewhere the landscape was modified considerably by 18th century improvers. The village of Edgcote itself was demolished and moved, and the hydrology of the area changed.

The River Cherwell on the northern edge of the Edgcote area is now a much different river. In particular its flow has been controlled by the construction of weirs and the holding of water in ponds on the Edgcote estate lands. The river was not, at the time of the battle, "20 feet wide and 2 feet deep"[13]. It should be noted that Edgcote is less than three miles from where Sir William Waller fought Charles Stuart at the Battle of Cropredy Bridge in June 1644. At that time, before the building of the weirs, Waller could only cross the Cherwell at two points, - Cropredy Bridge and the ford at Slats Mill, with a third crossing, Hays Bridge between Wardington and Chipping Warden, providing another choke point at the northern end of the battlefield. Hays Bridge is, in fact, less than two miles from Trafford Bridge, which has been placed by some writers as being on the battlefield, or at least provided passage for one or other of the armies across the River Cherwell and on to the battlefield. This must be borne in mind when considering the armies might have been manoeuvring in close proximity to each other. Depending on the size of the army, and how many men abreast it marched it could take anything from 10 minutes to half an hour to traverse either a bridge or

---

[9] This image can be seen online at http://cudl.lib.cam.ac.uk/view/PR-ATLAS-00002-00061-00001/1.
[10] OS Explorer Map 206 ref 520 467.
[11] Baker p500.
[12] The proposed HS2 line will provide a new railway line either on the eastern edge of the area, or right through the battlefield itself, depending upon the final decisions made on the construction and the interpretation of the evidence we have for the location of the battle.
[13] Bicheno, p122.

ford crossing for a river such as the Cherwell, during which time it would have been vulnerable to being attacked and defeated in detail.

Modern writers from Ramsay onwards have tended to cluster their locations for the battle around the area now known as Danes Moor and the hill with Edgcote Lodge Farm located at its eastern end, although there is debate about whether Pembroke's army faced South West[14], North East[15], North North East[16] South East[17] or simply East. We will look at each of these interpretations after we have considered what else the chroniclers tell us of the location.

Polydore Vergil, Guto'r Glyn and the writer of Hearne's Fragment give us no further clues, and Warkworth, the Croyland Continuator and John Stow go no further than just stating that the battle was fought on a plain. As we saw earlier, the contemporary Welsh poet, Lewis Glyn Cothi, however, not only confirmed the Banbury location but gave us a peak at some topographical detail, by telling us that the enemy were on a hill top.

Our earliest source for solid topographical details is Jean de Wavrin. He provides a fairly detailed account of several phases of fighting that take place across a "riviere". This is usually translated as "river", but actually means a tributary to a bigger river (where the word would be "fleuve"), - i.e. one that does not itself flow down to the sea. In this context it could refer to the Cherwell, which is a tributary of the River Thames at Oxford, but it could also refer to a waterway that feeds into the Cherwell itself. If de Wavrin is to be believed this is more likely to be the case because, as discussed above, the Cherwell was a major obstacle to movement at the time, and would be quite hard to fight across.

The relevance of de Wavrin's reference to the river is that the Danes Moor location does have a small river running through it, on the eastern edge, which eventually runs down through to the Cherwell. This watercourse is clearly visible on Speed's map of 1603, which was drawn before the landscape improvements of the 18th century. It also forms the eastern boundary of the Edgcote estate map discussed above and it can be clearly seen on the modern Ordnance Survey map. Modern walkers will not find it much of an obstacle, as it is overgrown and culverted in places, but its banks are clearly delineated by a meandering hedgerow.

It should come as no surprise that the most details provided by a single writer are in Hall. In addition to his naming of Hedgcote, he gives us the following details:

1) There are three hills
2) The hills are not "in equal distance"
3) The hills are not equal size
4) They lie in a manner "although not fully triangle"

---
[14] Ramsay, map facing p314.
[15] Bicheno, p124.
[16] Haigh "Where both the hosts" p44.
[17] Battlefield Trust website Resource Centre "Battle of Edgcote" (February 2019).

5) The Welsh were on the West Hill
6) The Welsh wanted to gain the East Hill as this would bring Victory.
7) The Northmen encamped on the South Hill
8) The battle was fought in the valley at the foot of the Welshmen's hill
9) Clapham's reinforcements come up the side of the East Hill.

These details have provided historians with a number of problems. In the general area of Edgcote there are many more than three hills, and many of them can be linked up to form a triangle, or not, depending on how Hall's words are read. The hills are also all helpfully not of equal size, and none of them is called East, West nor South, so these terms are only of help when referring to the hills relative to each other. The only possibly definite conclusion we can draw is that the East and West hills faced each other across a valley, which would place the South hill between and below them, so forming an inverted triangle, which may be what Hall's curious turn of phrase "although not fully triangle" means.

This all fits comfortably with the Danes Moor location, placing Pembroke on the Edgcote Lodge Hill, the Northmen on the ridge line to their east in the direction of Culworth and the other side of the stream. That would place the Northmen's camp in the area of Thorpe Mandeville. This makes complete sense if they had advanced from Northampton down the Banbury Lane, the old droving road and the most direct route between Northampton and Banbury.

If this is the case and the evidence all fits so neatly together, why do we have the multitude of orientations for the forming up of Pembroke's army which ultimately move the location of the actual fighting away from the stream and Danes Moor? It is possibly instructive to note that John Stow, writing after Hall and making use of his research, ignores completely all of Hall's information about the various hills.

Modern historians have struggled to make complete sense of all of the evidence when trying to fit it together. This problem is often solved by just referring to the battle as being a few miles outside Banbury and then reporting on the result. This is an approach followed, for example in Jacob's volume on the Fifteenth Century of the Oxford History of England, which barely gives the battle a line, the same as J R Lander's "The Wars of the Roses"[18] and Seward's work of the same name[19]. One honourable exception, which may come as a surprise, is Alison Weir's "Lancaster and York"[20], which devotes most of a page to a description of the location and fighting, based mostly upon de Wavrin.

There is not space here to go through all modern accounts of the battle and discuss their merits or otherwise. But it is instructive to look at four that all come to differing conclusions. Firstly we will look at Ramsay's account in "Lancaster and York", representing, as it does, the first modern application of scientific history to the subject.

---
[18] J R Lander "The Wars of the Roses" p126.
[19] D Seward "The Wars of the Roses" p159.
[20] A Weir "Lancaster & York" p351.

Secondly, Philip Haigh's account in "Where both the hosts fought", which is the most detailed account and the only monograph on the battle that has been published prior to this work. Thirdly it is useful to look at Hugh Bicheno's description in "Blood Royal" as an example of a modern, 21st century popular history book account. Finally we will consider the description given in Richard Brooks' "Cassell's Battlefields of Britain and Ireland" as the data from this book has been used elsewhere in this publication.

One of the first issues to look at is why, if the rebels are to the south of Pembroke's position, would they move up to the East Hill to fight a battle?

This conundrum exercised Ramsay considerably[21]. He has the rebels circle round the southern end of Pembroke's position on Edgcote Lodge Hill and attack them from the south west (see Ramsay's map below). The armies first confront each other on a frontage about 300 yards in length. Pembroke is then driven backwards down the slope behind him into Danes Moor where the final fighting takes place.

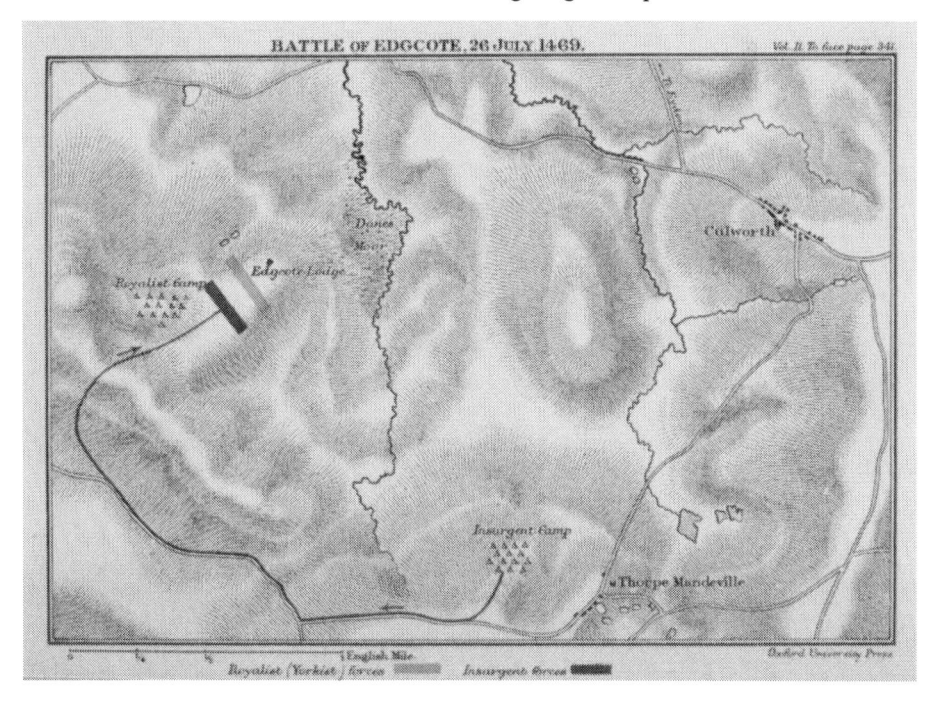

Map showing the final movement of the rebel army and the location of the battlefield, taken from Ramsay's "Lancaster & York".

---

[21] Ramsay p342. NB I have ignored Oman's account here as it is not entirely clear how it fits within the landscape.

There are a number of problems with this interpretation. The south western end of Pembroke's position is quite steep. The land falls from c175 metres to c150 metres in about 100 metres of distance. This is a gradient of 1 in 4, - more than enough in modern times to warrant the erection of a steep hill sign, with warnings to "Engage Low Gear Now" and forcing all but the fittest of cyclists to get off and walk. Pembroke's scouts and picquets must have been particularly lax to enable the rebels to force the position unopposed. Secondly, having forced Pembroke into the valley through archery the rebels have no incentive to descend after them and fight. The reference makes more sense if Pembroke descends the hill to engage the rebel army to force them to stop shooting at his army.

This interpretation also completely ignores de Wavrin's reference to fighting across the watercourse, with no explanation as to why it should be excluded. This is curious as earlier in his analysis of the developing crisis Ramsey uses de Wavrin's work in the discussion of the Duke of Clarence's wedding[22], and doubly so as the map included with the description of the battle clearly shows the river flowing from south to north, along the eastern edge of Danes Moor. Note here as well that Ramsay has moved Danes Moor slightly north and located it exclusively in the area now known as Danes Moor Spinney.

In practice there is no impediment to the rebels moving north, between the two hills directly above their camp in Ramsay's map, before turning west to advance over the east hill, and towards Danes Moor. This would enable them to attack Pembroke's army up the more gentle slope at the north eastern end of their position.

Haigh's account is detailed and supported by multiple maps[23]. A lot of his chapter on the battle is devoted to looking at the alternative theories before presenting a radical theory of his own.

The main driving force for his interpretation is that the rebels approached Edgcote from the direction of Daventry, and not down the Banbury Lane, and camped north of the River Cherwell the previous night in an area called Byfield Plain, next to Job's Hill. This is a logical location if the rebels did come from the direction of Daventry. In this interpretation the three hills are Job's Hill, Edgcote Lodge Hill and the collection of hills to the east, in the vicinity of Culworth.

As said above, this is a radical reinterpretation of the evidence. It should not be rejected out of hand, but it does raise a number of questions.

The first question is why would the rebels come down via Daventry, having fought the Royalist outriders near Northampton at the other end of Banbury Lane only a day or so before hand? The Daventry location turns upon one line in Hall, and a piece of interpretation in both Ramsay and Oman. After the skirmish near Northampton, Hall writes "The Yorke shire menne, beyng glad of this small victory, were well cooled

---

[22] Ramsay p336.
[23] Haigh "Where both the hosts" p32-53. Haigh's final position is shown on the map at the end of this chapter, together with the positions of the other theories being discussed.

and went no farther Southward, but toke their waie toward Warwicke, lokyng for aide of therle, whiche was lately come from Caleis".

Ramsay alters the sequence of events slightly and places this movement before the fight, and says "On nearing the enemy at some place whose name has not been recorded, *perhaps Daventry*, [my italics] Pembroke and Devon attempted a reconnaissance in force, but were repulsed"[24]. By the following page this has become not a "perhaps" but a certainty, and the armies are reported as marching down this axis. This analysis has passed into the historiography almost unquestioningly and therefore distorted subsequent writing. The problem here is that by accepting this statement in Hall it is necessary to ignore one of the others, - that the rebels camped on the southern hill. Regardless of how you look at it, Job's Hill is to the north of Edgcote Lodge Hill.

An "off road" stretch of Banbury Lane today. Some of the lane is still a modern, tarmac road. Photograph © Graham Evans.

The movements of the rebel army as reported is slightly confusing. Polydore Vergil, in one of his rare moments of detail for this campaign, seems to support Hall (or, rather, is one of Hall's sources) as he says that the Yorkshiremen were headed homeward as we saw in the previous chapter. Where is "homeward" in this context? Surely it does not mean Yorkshire, as he then goes on to say "mynding to stay whyle therle of

---
[24] Ramsay p340. Similar comments repeated in Oman p186.

Warweke should coome to them". Could it simply mean that they went back to their camp near Northampton?

The statement about the rebel army's movement in Hall is problematic. At this point Warwick was to the south of them, approaching from the south east, as he had only recently arrived from the continent. Not heading south but heading west towards Warwick (the place) does not bring the rebels closer to the Earl but in fact takes them further away (although, as we can see in the Coventry Leet Book, Warwick was hoping to add Coventry's archers to his army, but as he was arguing that he was going to use them to fight the rebels he would hardly be in a position to send the rebel army to pick them up).

Trying to make sense of Hall's description of this movement is difficult if we want to make all of the bits relevant. We are hampered by not knowing what Hall's source was. A possible interpretation is that Hall is repeating a garbled verbal report and that it should refer to Warwick the person, not Warwick the place[25], and that the reference to not going further south was added later to justify the movement.

Edgcote Lodge Hill looking north. The River Cherwell is behind the trees in the distance, and Trafford Bridge to the right. Photograph © Graham Evans

There is very little way in fact that movement from Daventry is compatible with the army camping on a hill south of the Royalist position.

The next problem with this interpretation is that the area identified for the battle isn't on Danes Moor. The area commonly accepted to be Danes Moor runs to the west of the tributary to the Cherwell, from the foot of Edgcote Lodge Hill up to Trafford Bridge and encompassing Danes Moor Spinney. The southern end is now taken up by the Edgcote National Hunt racecourse. Haigh places the battle to the north of Edgcote

---
[25] I owe this observation to Phil Steele.

Lodge Hill, with Pembroke's army on the high ground facing north north east, and the rebels below them with their back to the Cherwell, having crossed the river in the Trafford Bridge area, and marched across the front of Pembroke's army before deploying. This seems to be unlikely, or at the very least, quite dangerous, firstly to make a river crossing with the enemy within a mile and then to march into position with a flank exposed until fully deployed. The rebels knew that Pembroke's force had cavalry, having been attacked by them at Northampton. Also the night before the battle there was skirmishing that saw Sir Henry Neville killed, so a surprise attack whilst performing this manoeuvre would have been distinctly possible.

This location also means that de Wavrin's evidence of the fighting across the river has to be rejected (as indeed, Haigh does[26]) unless it refers to the initial fighting over the crossing point on the site of Trafford Bridge.

The final problem with this interpretation is that it cannot be construed as placing the rebels on the East Hill, so the Welsh gaining that hill would not give them victory. In fact, the rebels aren't on a hill at all, which discounts Lewis Glyn Cothi's very precise description of the enemy being on a hill top. As we will see in Chapter 5 there are good reasons for believing that factual statements in a Welsh elegy are likely to be accurate.

Hugh Bicheno's account[27] is lively and atmospheric, and relies heavily on Haigh's analysis. He, too, accepts the advance from Daventry but rejects Haigh's placement of the armies. The accompanying map has the armies facing each other across the northern end of Danes Moor, with Pembroke's men at the extreme eastern end of Edgcote Lodge Hill, deployed facing north east. The rebels have their right flank anchored on the Cherwell, and face Pembroke's men across the small river discussed earlier. They are on the lower slopes, such as they are, of the two hills opposite Edgcote Lodge Hill.

This deployment solves the issue of the rebels having to march across Pembroke's front to deploy, and also allows them to be on hilly ground to the east of the Royalists. In order to deal with the difficulty of forcing the crossing over the Cherwell Bicheno has relied upon the nature of the river at this point being the same as it is now, and therefore readily fordable on a reasonably wide frontage, relying on the crossing point at Trafford Bridge purely for wheeled transport, if they had any. As we have seen above, this was not the case, and even as late as the 17th century the Cherwell was a sufficient barrier to movement to present English Civil War armies with difficulties.

Finally we turn to Brooks[28]. He ignores completely any idea that the armies came via Daventry and points to the medieval road system which passed through Northampton and the importance of Banbury Lane, that connects Northampton and Banbury. He places the final action to the south of Danes Moor, on the site of the modern Edgcote National Hunt racecourse. He has the rebels camped at Thorpe

---
[26] Haigh "Where both the hosts" p114-5.
[27] Bicheno p122-126.
[28] Brooks p255-257.

Mandeville (as did Ramsay) and attack Edgcote Lodge Hill directly, rather than pass round to the south, before scaling the steep slope. This interpretation is virtually identical to that proposed by the Battlefields Trust on their website.

The main issue with this interpretation is that it required Brooks to shift the fight across the river described in de Wavrin – who Brooks describes as "the best contemporary source" – to the night before, and also up to Trafford Bridge although he gives no explanation as to why an army coming from Banbury would need to dispute a crossing at Trafford Bridge against an army coming down the Banbury Lane, - and also, of course, provides no reason for why gaining the East Hill would provide victory if attacked from the south.

To enable as much of the evidence to fit as we can all that is required is for the rebel attack to come from the direction of Culworth, with their overnight camp being in the vicinity of Thorpe Mandeville[29]. In respect of de Wavrin the armies face each other over the tributary, and as for Hall's evidence:

1) There are three hills – Edgcote Lodge Hill ("West Hill"), the hill at Thorpe Mandeville ("South Hill") and the hill facing Edgcote Lodge across Danes Moor ("East Hill")
2) The hills are not "in equal distance" – from "West Hill" to "East Hill" is just under half a mile, from "East Hill" to "South Hill" about a mile and from "South Hill" to "West Hill" about a mile and a half.
3) The hills are not equal size – "West Hill" rises to 179 metres, "East Hill" 142 metres and "South Hill" 173 metres.
4) They lie in a manner "although not fully triangle" – the three hills form an inverted, rather squashed triangle.
5) The Welsh were on the "West Hill" - this fits with advancing up from Banbury and camping on Edgcote Lodge Hill.
6) The Welsh wanted to gain the "East Hill" as this would bring victory - capturing the "East Hill" would mean the defeat of the rebels who initially deployed there.
7) The Northmen encamped on the "South Hill" - the "South Hill" is just off the Banbury Lane, the route the rebels would have taken from Northampton.
8) The battle was fought in the valley at the foot of the Welshmen's hill – Danes Moor is at the foot of Edgcote Lodge Hill.
9) Clapham's reinforcements come up the side of the "East Hill" – advancing over the side of the "East Hill", either north of it or south of it, would follow the most direct route from Northampton to Edgcote and Danes Moor.

The proposed location fulfils all of Hall's criteria, and in addition has the added benefit of including the detail we get from de Wavrin. It would seem, therefore, that we can be fairly certain of the location of the battle, and it was where we had been told

---

[29] Maps showing the locations of the armies are given in Chapter 7, along with a description of the fighting.

all along. There should have been no need for an ingenious interpretation of the evidence we have been left, we simply need to trust what was written after the event.

The exact sequence of events of the fighting, however, need to be looked at in greater detail, and we will turn to them in Chapter 7.

Edgcote Lodge Hill ("West Hill") from the East Hill. The line of the stream is marked by the hedge line. Danes Moor is just beyond that. Photograph © Graham Evans

East Hill from Danes Moor, looking north east. Bicheno's battlefield site is further to the left. De Wavrin's stream is the hedge line at the foot of the hill. Photograph © Graham Evans

43

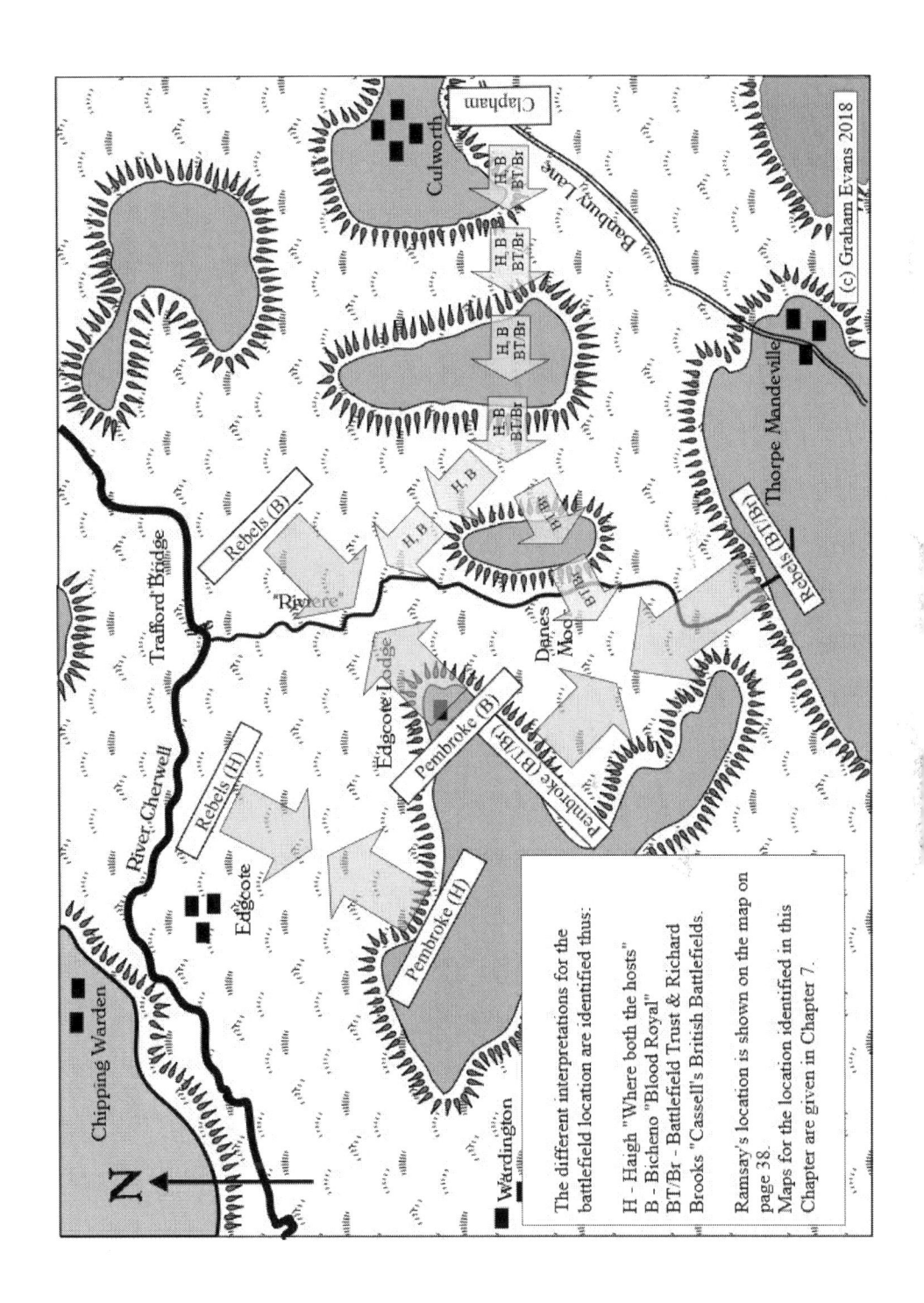

Chapter 5 - Naming the Day

One thing we do have in several of our sources is a good, clear, statement of when the battle was fought. We are lucky in that it was fought on or around a Saint's day, - St James' Day to be precise. As we know when that day is in the Church's calendar - the 25th July - we can be reasonably certain as to when the battle was fought.

So why did the Institute of Historical Research Bulletin feel the need to publish a short article called "The Exact Date of the Battle of Banbury" in 1982[1]? Is there any doubt about when the battle was actually fought? As we saw earlier[2] we have good chronicler evidence for the date of the battle being the 26th July.

However, there is a possibility of error. What we do *not* have is any official records dating the battle. That's because neither the King, nor Warwick, nor Clarence (probably) were present. As we will see later we have good records for where the King was at various times during the campaign, because he writes letters to people with dates on them, or he issues instructions to departments of the Royal Households, again with dates on them. These are kept in the Royal Archives, or, in the case of some correspondence, we have letters

The Battlefield Trust onsite sign board shows the date unequivocally as the 26th July, but is it correct?
Photograph © Graham Evans

in the Coventry Leet Book. (What the latter tells us is that Edward was in Nottingham on the 29th July, but where he had been in the weeks beforehand is not certain).

Similarly with the manifestos and statements of Warwick. We have evidence for them in official records that can place him and Clarence at certain times. They are in Calais on the 11th July for Clarence and Isabel's wedding, for example. What we do not have is a letter or statement from Warwick or Clarence, announcing that they have triumphed personally over the evil councillors corrupting the King because the fact is that they did not as they weren't at the battle. Warwick's involvement in deposing the evil advisors and upstart councillors is his instigation of the series of rather grubby and legally questionable summary executions of his opponents.

---

[1] Lewis, W.G. (1982b), 'The Exact Date of the Battle of Banbury, 1469', *Bulletin of the Institute of Historical Research*, LV: 194–6. This chapter draws heavily on this article and also Dr Barry Lewis' "The Battle of Edgcote or Banbury (1469) through the eyes of Contemporary Welsh Poets" Journal of Medieval Military History: Volume IX (2011).

[2] Chapter 1, Footnote 6.

In the absence of any official records we must fall back upon our chroniclers to determine the date. And the date of the battle is important as it is in respect of that date that other events can be dated. Alas not all of our chroniclers give us any dating evidence. De Wavrin, for example gives us no dating evidence at all.

In respect of the English chroniclers some of our earliest dating evidence comes from Warkworth's Chronicle. This gives "the xxvj. day of Juylle" as the date for the battle, which seems to be, on the face of it, completely unambiguous. The Croyland Chroniclers give us nothing, and neither does the writer of Hearne's Fragment. Polydore Vergil is similarly unhelpful. Hall then fixes the date for us as the day after Saint James' Day. Or, to be precise, he says that the argument over lodgings in Banbury takes place on Saint James' Day, and the battle on the morning after, before later saying "the morrow after sainct James daye" This date is confirmed in Stow, although, of course, we know that he used Hall as a source, so again we could have copying not corroboration.

We can see from this that amongst these English sources we have consensus, although admittedly it is possible that we only have two sources, and it might even be only one, if Hall had visited Cambridge and read Warkworth's work.

There are however "English" sources that give us a different date for the battle. One of these is the anonymous chronicle that we have referred to as the "Brief Latin Chronicle". This quite clearly and unambiguously places the battle on the day before the Feast of Saint James[3], or the 24th July. Furthermore, the Coventry Leet Book, in a Latin Memorandum, also gives us the eve of Saint James' Day, although the editor[4] of the published version states in a footnote "Authorities declare 26th July to have been the date", without saying who the authorities are.

It would appear, therefore, that the English sources that give a date are equally divided on whether the battle was fought before or after the Feast of St James, but that those which are the most contemporary, - for the Coventry Leet Book was written and compiled contemporaneously with the events it covers,- favouring the earlier date.

Perhaps we can break the deadlock by turning to the Welsh poets, a source that seems to provide difficulties for non-Welsh historians. As stated above there are two very useful articles written on Edgcote by two scholars of the Welsh Language and poetry. (NB Some, but not all, of the poems they quote from are included, some with new translations, in the Primary Sources Appendix at the end of this book.)

The most well known of the Welsh poems about the battle is the elegy written by Guto'r Glyn for William Herbert. This doesn't give any actual dates, and due to its poetic structure has provided difficulties for historians trying to make it fit with the overall sequence of events leading up to the battle. However, it does make reference to the days of the week on which things occurred, and gives us this couplet that identifies when the battle was fought:

---

[3] "in vigilia Sancti Jacobi Apostoli".
[4] Mary Dormer Harris 1867 - 1936, a writer and historian, and thoroughly remarkable woman.

Duw Llun y bu waed a lladd,	On Monday there was blood and slaughter,
Dydd amliw, diwedd ymladd	a day of disgrace, the end of all fighting.

The 26th of July in 1469 was not a Monday; it was a Wednesday. Guto'r Glyn was therefore writing about the eve of the Feast of Saint James. Haigh acknowledges the problem with Guto'r Glyn referring to a Monday when fighting took place, but resolves the issue by concluding that the lines refer to the earlier skirmish, not the actual battle[5]. This interpretation is unlikely, as the poem references "the end of all fighting", which would be an unusual use of language if there was fighting on subsequent days. The question might be asked as to why we would rely upon the work of a poet over those of men who regarded themselves as historians or chroniclers of their times.

That approach is to misunderstand the role of the Welsh poet in the late medieval age. It isn't an accident that Guto'r Glyn wrote an elegy for William Herbert. He wrote many poems for the family, and would have been commissioned to write this elegy probably to be recited at "the month's mind", a service of remembrance held a month after the funeral[6]. This provides extra evidence that the day used in the poem is correct for the date of the battle. As Lewis remarks *"It is not credible that these poets could stand up in public ceremonies, before not only the dead men's families but also their retainers, supporters and neighbours, men in a position to know the facts, and announce that the fateful battle was fought on Monday, the eve of St. James's Day, if it had actually been fought on Wednesday, the day after St. James's Day*[7]*."*

If that is not enough, then both W G & B Lewis quote from a total of four poets, including Guto'r Glyn, who all state that the battle was fought on a Monday. Two of them even go as far as to refer to "noswyl Iago", or the Eve of James.

Unlike the English sources those Welsh sources that have become known to us, - which apparently include a mid 16th century chronicle in Welsh, quoted by W G Lewis - are unequivocal about the date of the battle. Let us not forget that this battle had a deep impact on the Welsh psyche at the time. The evidence that we have is that nearly a whole generation of Welsh nobility was wiped out in a day. What may appear to the English in retrospect as a battle that caused an intermission in the rule of Edward IV was a national disaster in Wales[8]. It is not a date that high profile Welsh poets were going to get wrong, for to do so would have invited ridicule.

What is remarkable is that given the weight of the evidence, both English and Welsh, that the date of the battle is the 24th of July, not the 26th, is that the latter date has persisted in written accounts. It is a testimony to the influence of Ramsay and Hall, as discussed earlier, that historians are unable to bring themselves to write down a different date, and the otherwise redoubtable Mary Dormer Harris was caused to

---

[5] Haigh, "Where both the hosts" p32.
[6] B Lewis JMMH IX p98.
[7] B Lewis JMMH IX p105.
[8] H T Evans p108.

disbelieve the evidence of her own eyes during her decade-long work on the Coventry Leet Book. Even the classic work "Wales and the Wars of the Roses", written in 1915 by the Welsh scholar, H T Evans, who had access to the poems we have been discussing and used them extensively omits Guto'r Gyn's reference to the fateful Monday, - perhaps because he believes that Monday was the 23rd, not the 24th July[9]. He compounds this error with the mistranslation of the line 7 of Guto'r Glyn's poem "Duw a ddug y dydd dduw Iau" as "The field was lost on Thursday"[10] instead of "On Thursday God took away", before referring to the execution of William Herbert contained in the following line. Only one modern historian has taken on board W G Lewis' findings, and that is Michael Hicks in his biography "Warwick the Kingmaker", and he states the fact almost as a throw away line - *"Finding Edward's forces divided, the northerners fell on Pembroke's Welshmen at Edgecote on 24 July and destroyed them"*[11].

We can only speculate on why Hall's work contains the reference to Saint James' Day. The only source we know he could have consulted that uses that date is the Warkworth Chronicle, which does not reference Saint James' Day (which is, in itself, odd, in such a pious society) but writes it in Roman numerals "xxvj. day of Juylle". It would not have taken much to transpose the last two characters of the number to give us xxjv, or twenty four. If Hall had seen Warkworth's work, then it is he who chooses to give the date by reference to the Saint's day rather than drawing it from a source, as there are no sources that give the battle as being dated the day after St James' Day in those terms. Those who use St James' Day as a reference point quite clearly use the Latin word for the day before a Saint's Day "vigilia". It is quite difficult to put that down to the medieval equivalent of a typographical error, unlike the writing of a date in roman numerals.

The last point to consider in this discussion is the death of William Herbert. Most chroniclers give it as shortly after the battle, but are no more precise than that, except for Polydore Vergil, who tells us that the beheadings took place two days later. That would place them on the Wednesday the 26th, if the Welsh poets are correct, or Friday the 28th, if we favour Hall. In fact, Guto'r Glyn and two of his contemporaries set the day for Pembroke's execution as Thursday, the 27th July[12]. If Polydore Vergil is correct, therefore, the battle was fought on the 25th. However, it would be placing an enormous amount of reliance on one piece of evidence in Polydore Vergil to overturn evidence and references in what we can now see are at least half a dozen contemporary, independent sources. Given Polydore Vergil's track record in respect of the Edgcote campaign and the battle in particular that would be acting in the face of all logic.

---

[9] H T Evans p104. Evans has the days and dates incorrect for the entire week. We can perhaps forgive him as he did not have access to internet day of the week checkers.
[10] H T Evans p162, note 70.
[11] Hicks p271 and 277.
[12] W G Lewis p195, B Lewis p106.

It seems, therefore, that we must conclude that the Welsh academics who have studied their native sources for this battle are correct, and can state, confidently, that the battle was fought on the 24th July.

The challenge now is to try to change the date in the historiographical record.

Chapter 6 - "I am Robin of Redesdale!"

The 1469 revolt that led to the capture of the then King of England is a pivotal point in the history of late 15th century England, and the victory of the army of Northerners, led by Robin of Redesdale[1], over a formidable force under William Herbert, one of the King's favourites, must rate as one of the most successful popular rebellions in English history. Of course, it would appear that the rising that led to the Battle of Edgcote was not just or only a simple popular uprising. The fingerprints of Richard Neville, the Earl of Warwick, the "Kingmaker" are all over it[2].

Whilst we can confidently comment upon how it was Warwick who was the mastermind behind it all, what we are less certain of is who was Warwick's man in the North. Indeed, was it Warwick's man, or was it a genuine populist leader who provided Warwick with the opportunity to piggyback on the disruption he was causing?

What is certain is that Robin of Redesdale was a pseudonym, and one used by more than one person, possibly over a period of years. In addition we have several other "Robin" characters raising rebellion amongst the common folk, and going not just by the name of Robin of Redesdale. We also have Robin Mend-all[3], or Robin of Holderness, Robert de Redysdale, and sometimes Robert Hulderne although this latter might be an actual name, rather than a pseudonym.

The name presumably had meaning for the people of the time and was not chosen at random. Keith Dockray, in his article on the 1469 Yorkshire Rebellions, is not the only person to have drawn the link with Robin Hood and the use of the name Robin as a leader or avenger of the poor. The choice of Redesdale as a soubriquet for a rebel leader in Yorkshire may also have some significance lost to us now. Redesdale is not in Yorkshire, but is in Northumberland, up by the Scottish border, with all that entails for lawlessness and taking the law into your own hands. It is over 100 miles from York, the site of the initial rising that ended at the gates of that City, and nearly a 150 miles from Doncaster, the supposed launch point for the rebels' sally into the southern counties of England. The Lord of Redesdale at the time was Robert, 1st Baron Ogle, who was also the Warden of the East March, a man who had survived the vagaries of both border and Northern politics and should probably be counted as part of the Neville affinity. It may just be that "Redesdale" is intended to signify a tough outsider who is prepared to do what it takes to get justice for the common man, and perhaps if the actual individual is a local man it does no harm to imply that you are not from round the area when the forces of law and order come to call.

The Yorkshire risings of 1469 are confusing in themselves in that we know there were more than one, and that they may have had slightly different aims. The

---

[1] There are several forms of "Redesdale" in the sources: Rissedalle, Ryddesdale, Redysdale, Riddesdale, Riddisdale, and Ridsedale, but Redesdale is the commonly accepted modern spelling.
[2] For example see the terms of the rebel's manifesto in the Appendix, which is a duplicate of that issued by Clarence and Warwick.
[3] Dockray, "Yorkshire Rebellions" p2.

Chroniclers of the period seem uncertain as to the exact sequence of events, and the actions in several revolts may have been conflated, and also the actions of more than one leader. This complexity has received thorough treatment at the hands of Keith Dockray in the article mentioned earlier, and also in Haigh's book on Edgcote[4].

It is not always clear when our chroniclers are writing about Robin whether they are writing about the same person in each of the rebellions, - not surprising when sometimes they cannot determine if there is one rebellion or several.

Luckily for us the identity or actual existence of the Robins that precede the Edgcote campaign are not of great importance in respect of the Robin who ends up in Northamptonshire in 1469. Their existence signifies that the north of England was in turmoil at the time, but the ubiquity and low level of disturbance may explain Edward's tardiness in collecting his army, or perhaps it was his trust in Warwick's brother, John Neville, the Earl of Northumberland as the man whose job it was to keep law and order in the northern counties. This trust may appear to have been well founded, at least initially, as one of the rebels, identified by Hall (probably based upon Polydore Vergil) as Robert Hulderne was captured and beheaded by Northumberland at the gates of York. Hulderne had been leading a revolt over practices at the charitable hospital of Saint Leonard's in York, and the full details of the grievances are given in the extract from Hall in the Primary Sources Appendix of this book.

Alas no date is given for this in Hall, but we do have some other evidence that ties this event to Robin of Redesdale. The records of Beverley Corporation note that they sent mounted archers to the support of Northumberland on the morrow St Mark's Day[5], and that they served for nine days. St Mark's Day is the 25th April, so the suppression of the rebellion and the execution probably took place in early May. The "Brief Latin Chronicle" also refers to Robin of Redesdale raising an army about this time, and shortly afterwards also Robin of Holderness, who is then beheaded by Northumberland.

If this all took place in April and May and ended with the death of the rebel leader, who may or may not have been using the name of Robin of Redesdale, there is a clear break until trouble starts again at the end of June, leading to the Battle of Edgcote.

Several chroniclers give us names for some of the leaders of the rebels, and historians have speculated on who the real Robin of Redesdale was, starting in the 16th century, even up to today. The merits of the case for whether or not each one was Robin of Redesdale are discussed below.

"Lord Willoughby"

The first chronicler to give us a leader's name is de Wavrin who says that the rebels were led by "le comte de Wilbie" which is usually read as "Lord Willoughby." This could refer to either Sir Richard Welles (1428 - 1470)[6], who was married to the 7th Baroness Willoughby de Eresby, or his son, Sir Robert Welles (1446 - 1470), 8th Baron

---

[4] Haigh "Where both the hosts"p16-31.
[5] "pro repressione Hob. De Redesdale" - for the suppression of Hob de Redesdale.
[6] Dates of birth and death are taken from a variety of internet genealogy sites.

Willoughby de Eresby. The Welles' held lands in Lincolnshire and the family were Lancastrians turned Yorkists. Both are better known for being amongst the leaders of the rebellion that ended at Losecote Field on the 12th March 1470[7]. Sir Richard was executed on the day of the "battle" before it started, and his son was captured and executed at Doncaster a week later. Whilst it is possible that de Wavrin has mixed up stories of the two rebellions in different years, there is no reason why Welles could not also have been at Edgcote the previous year[8]. Lincolnshire is closely linked to South Yorkshire and Doncaster where the rebels set out from, according to Guto'r Glyn. The Welles family also held lands in Yorkshire.

Having gone to this trouble to show that either or both of the Welles could have been at Edgcote, the candidacy as Robin of Redesdale is less certain, as de Wavrin does not name him as such, but merely remarks that "Those from the North were lead by Lord Willoughby, accompanied by a villain called Robin of Rissedale, captain of all the common people", stating unambiguously, in effect, that they were two different people.

Sir William Conyers (1435 -1475)

Warkworth's chronicle clearly names Sir William Conyers as Robin of Redesdale, when it says: "Sere William Conyars knyghte was therre capteyne, whiche callede hym self Robyne of Riddesdale". Sir William Conyers of Marske was an indentured retainer of the Earl of Warwick[9] (as were all the Conyers we will discuss here), and a cousin by marriage, with lands in Yorkshire, and so is an eligible candidate for the role of the rebel's leader if he was a Warwick nominee. William was the son of the elder Sir John Conyers, and younger brother of the other, who are discussed below. Despite the unequivocal statement that William was Robin, some modern writers are prepared to accept Warkworth's account of what happened, but only if one of the other Conyers is substituted[10] or dismissed entirely on the grounds of insufficient experience[11].

Sir John Conyers, (c1411 - 1490)

Sir John Conyers of Hornby[12], another indentured retainer of the Earl of Warwick, is named as one of the rebel leaders first by Hall, where he is noted to be the "tutor and governor" to two young men who were regarded as captains of the rebels, Sir Henry Fitzhugh and Sir Henry Neville. He is also said to be a man of great courage and valour, rarely matched at the time. Hall records that he was present at the execution of Sir William Herbert, and turned down the latter's request for clemency for his younger brother. It is interesting to note in Hall's account that the name "Robyn of

---

[7] See Haigh "Where both the hosts" p67 - 84.
[8] T Coveney. Vol 2 H-R, p21-22.
[9] T Coveney Vol 3 S-Y p33.
[10] E.g. See Weir, p350.
[11] Bicheno p114.
[12] T Coveney Vol 3 S-Y p32.

Riddesdale" is not adopted by the captain of the commons until *after* the executions of the Herbert brothers. This means that in the most detailed account of the Edgcote campaign that we have Robin of Redesdale is *not* the leader of the rebels. Stow includes "Sir John Coniers, Knight" as one of the leaders of the Northern host, but has him working alongside Robert of Hilliard, who named himself "Robin of Ridesdale". In that way, as with Lord Willoughby above, some of the sources most definitely tell us that he is not Robin of Redesdale.

(Sir) John (James) Conyers, (c1433 - 1469)

The other Sir John Conyers, in addition to being an indentured Neville family retainer, had family links to Warwick through his marriage to Alice Neville, the daughter of the Earl of Warwick's uncle, William Neville. He comes to our notice in both Warkworth and Stow, both of whom record him in virtually identical wording, calling him "James Coniers, sonne and heire to Sir John Coniers, knight". As other casualties are referred to as "Sir" it may be that John/James had not been knighted at the time of the battle.[13] His name is never linked with Robin of Redesdale, nor is he mentioned by anyone as one of the rebels' leaders. It seems unlikely that he would have been in overall charge of the rebels in the presence of his father.

Sir Henry Fitzhugh, 5th Lord Fitzhugh (1424 - 1472)

Described by Hall as a "young man" guided by his tutor, Sir John Conyers, Fitzhugh was actually in his mid forties at the time of the battle. He is only mentioned as one of the captains of the rebels by Hall, and not in the context of being Robin of Redesdale,[14] nor overall leader, due to the presence of his old tutor, Sir John Conyers. As such he does not seem to be a strong candidate to be Robin. NB He is listed amongst the dead recorded by William of Worcester, but not on anyone else's casualty roll and seems to still be alive after the battle and was involved in the 1470 rising as well[15].

Sir Henry Neville (1437 - 1469)

The son of George Neville, 1st Baron Latimer, Sir Henry Neville was Warwick's cousin. He is listed by Hall as one of the young men (and at 32, that just about fits) who was a leader of the rebels, but as with Henry Fitzhugh not in the context of being the overall leader or Robin of Redesdale. He is also referred to as Henry Latimer, or Lord Latimer in the chronicles. It is fairly certain that these are references to Sir Henry Neville as his father was mentally incapacitated at the time[16], and his son, Richard Latimer, was only 1 year old. He is recorded as dying either in a skirmish the day

---

[13] Most genealogist websites refer to him as "Sir John", and so conclude that he had been knighted. However, at least one refers to him as "Sir John 'Robin Hood' Conyers", so the reader can judge the reliability for themselves.

[14] But note, as stated above, Hall does not mention Robin of Redesdale until he is chosen by the men of Northamptonshire and the North after the battle.

[15] T Coveney Vol 3 S-Y p34.

[16] Burkes Peerage 1949, p1169.

before, (Hall) or at the battle (Hearne, Stow and William Worcestre). He was sufficiently well regarded by the rebels for his death to be a reason to deny clemency to Sir Richard Herbert (Hall). From the evidence we have in Hall he appears to be a commander of light horse.

Robert of Hilliard

Robert of Hilliard is recorded in Stow as being Robin of Redesdale. He has been identified as being Sir Robert Hildyard of Wynestead[17] (c1436 - 1501), in preference to his father of the same name (c1416 - c1485/9). Winestead is in the Holderness district of East Yorkshire, and the Hildyards were Lancastrians and members of the Percy affinity, Robert being knighted by Henry Percy in 1482. This makes him a good candidate for the Robin of Holderness in the "Brief Latin Chronicle", which, however, also makes it clear that this is a different person to Robin of Redesdale. As Robin of Holderness campaigned for the restitution of the legitimate heir of the Earl of Northumberland (ie for a Percy to replace the incumbent Neville holder) it seems unlikely that he would be the key man in a Neville backed uprising. The Hildyards are only reconciled to the Yorkist cause following the death of Warwick and the acceptance of Edward IV's monarchy by the Percy family.

There is a further issue in citing Hilliard as Holderness, in that it is reported in the "Brief Latin Chronicle" that he is beheaded by the Earl of Northumberland and as can be seen from the dates above both father and son lived past 1469.

Robert Hulderne[18]

Robert Hulderne is named by Polydore Vergil as the leader of the rebels who marched on York in the dispute over the paying of "first fruits" to the Hospital of St Leonards. As he is reported as having his head struck off by "the marquyse, lyuetenant of that countrye" (i.e. John Neville, Earl of Northumberland), he is unlikely to have been the Robin of Redesdale at the Battle of Edgcote. This story is repeated in Hall, but without giving the rebel captain's name. As we know from the Corporation of Beverley records archers were sent to fight "Hob of Redesdale" under the Earl of Northumberland at the same time as the "Brief Latin Chronicle" says Redesdale was active. Hulderne could therefore be a different person to Hilliard/Hildyard, and either one, both or neither of them were executed by the Earl of Northumberland. It is possible that if he survived then the Robin of Redesdale outside York is the same Robin of Redesdale at Northampton. It should be noted, however, that there is a three month gap between the rising around York, which is dated to the end of April and the Battle of Edgcote at the end of July. That is a long time to keep a peasant revolt style army in being.

---

[17] T Coveney Vol 3 S-Y p37.
[18] For the point of view that Hulderne and Hilliard are the same person, see Haigh "Where both the hosts", Appendix III. I have been unable to confirm his reference in Poulson's History of Holderness that links Hulderne and Hilliard/Hildyard.

Lord Robert Ogle (1406 - 1469)

Lord Robert Ogle, 1st Baron Ogle, Warden of the East March and Lord of Redesdale is not mentioned in any of the sources as being a candidate for Robin of Redesdale. His case is made for him by Hugh Bicheno in "Blood Royal"[19]. Bicheno's case, other than that Ogle was a senior and trusted Neville retainer, is based on two main points:

1) He was Lord of Redesdale.
2) He was a more experienced military commander than any of the other candidates.

Ogle's presence at the battle is confirmed in Bicheno's account by the statement that he is mortally wounded in the fighting, although no contemporary or near contemporary source gives him as one of the casualties[20].

As an attempt to conceal identity "Robin of Redesdale" is a fairly poor effort if the individual is actually from Redesdale. Especially as, in the Croyland Chronicle account the name is given as "**Robert** of Redesdale". Perhaps the name is not a pseudonym at all. Having said that, Robert Ogle was a prominent man in the North of England, and the absence of an overt reference to him in any chronicle is odd.

As for military experience, four of the candidates for Robin of Redesdale's mantle have no recorded military experience in previous battles or campaigns. These are the younger Sir John Conyers, Sir William Conyers, Sir Robert Hildyard and Sir Robert Welles. The others were present at the following battles[21]:

Lord Robert Ogle:	1st St Albans, Blore Heath, 2nd St Albans, Towton
Sir John Conyers:	1st St Albans, Blore Heath, Northampton, Towton
Sir Henry Fitzhugh:	Wakefield, 2nd St Albans, Towton
Sir Richard Welles:	Wakefield, 2nd St Albans, Towton, Hexham
Sir Henry Neville:	Hedgeley Moor, Hexham

Even without Ogle, it would appear that Conyers, Fitzhugh, Welles and Neville all had sufficient experience to conduct military operations.

Having had a look at the possible candidates, what conclusions can be drawn? When considering the true nature of Robin of Redesdale for the purposes of this book we are interested in the Robin of Redesdale who ended up at Edgcote in July 1469 and is associated with the manifesto that so closely mirrors that of the Earl of Warwick. To that extent the contradictory evidence of the rising round York in April is of less interest because we can be fairly confident that regardless of executions or otherwise we do end up with a Robin of Redesdale in South Northamptonshire.

---

[19] Bicheno p114.
[20] It should be noted that the Dictionary of National Biography gives his date of death as 1st November 1469.
[21] Information taken from T Coveney, Vols 1-3.

There are three ways of looking at the Robin of Redesdale problem, or perhaps three scenarios that might explain him. These might be termed the "Pulp", "Batman" and "Spartacus" scenarios.

1) The "Pulp" Scenario

   What if Robin of Redesdale is what some of our chroniclers claim? What if he was a member of the "Common People"? Rebel leaders of this sort were not without precedent at the time. In the previous hundred years Jack Cade had led a peasants revolt in 1450, and Wat Tyler the same in 1381. Not much is known about Cade or Tyler as they were both of common birth. It is possible that the search for a known individual to place behind the Robin of Redesdale mask is futile. He may possibly have actually been of non-noble birth, and was genuinely a local rascal or villain. If this is the case it might be, as de Wavrin, Hall and Stow imply, that Robin of Redesdale was in charge of the mob whilst the men discussed above were present with their affinities running what might be called the professional part of the rising. To that extent the hunt for who Robin of Redesdale was is intriguing but ultimately futile, and the rascal's attempt to conceal his identity was and is a success over 500 years later. In this case Robin is to be applauded for the efficacy of his efforts to remain anonymous.

2) The "Batman" Scenario

   Most historians have pursued this scenario. i.e. that they need to find the person who is to Robin of Redesdale as Bruce Wayne is to Batman. The evidence as we have seen is sometimes clear, but not entirely believable, or is contradictory. Sir William Conyers is clearly stated as being Robin, but his youth and lack of experience in the presence of his father and older brother makes him an unlikely leader. Halls' case for the older Sir John Conyers to be the overall leader then looks more convincing, and there is no need to add Lord Ogle into the mix to provide grey hairs and military experience. Although, of course, in Hall's narrative Conyers may be the leader, but he is not Robin of Redesdale.

3) The "Spartacus" Scenario

   In this scenario, in reference to the end of the film, Robin of Redesdale is not one individual, - or at least not all the time - but represents a figurehead[22]. Medieval armies often operated with a council of war, even when a king was present. In the case of the Northern rebels they have no senior large magnate present. Warwick may have been sending instructions but he was not there in person. The names of the captains discussed above probably represent the collective leadership of the rebel group, with one of their number acting as Robin when required. This would have made it easier to find another "Robin" in the event of his unfortunate demise.

---

[22] I owe this idea to a number of conversations with Phil Steele. The decision to call it "The Spartacus Scenario", however, is all my own.

If this was the case, then the hunt for a single individual to take Robin's identity is to miss the point entirely.

What this review of the evidence shows is that it is possible for a historian to make a good case for any one of several people for being Robin at any particular point in time. It is easier, perhaps to argue who it is not, rather than who it is and anyone who expresses absolute certainty on the evidence pointing to a specific individual is probably unwise to do so.

Although, I suspect, it will not stop anyone trying again in the future.

Chapter 7 - The Most Mighty Battlefield

Having looked at where it was fought and when, and how many men were present, it is now time to look in detail at what happened on the Vigil of St James over 500 years ago, and the days beforehand.

It will be apparent from what has gone before that this will not be straight forward. The sources do not align perfectly, and matters of detail are spread across multiple chroniclers and poets. Again there seems to be an evolution of the account over time, before, as always, it reaches its final form in the account of Hall. It will already have been evident from the discussion about the location of the battle that modern historians have placed the battle in a variety of positions in the area around Edgcote. The belief of what is important in our sources and what is not has influenced these interpretations as does making the accounts of what happened actually fit into the landscape.

What is clear from the accounts of several historians is that some severe surgery may have to take place on the chroniclers' events and chronology in order to make sense of it all. Actions are moved to different days, for example, or maybe actions on different days need to be combined. In the case of some writers they have taken the simple course of either ignoring or relying exclusively on one of the major sources.

In the absence of a detailed contemporary description, backed up with video footage and definitive archaeology any account of the battle will contain an amount of conjecture. In some ways we think we can be sure of more negatives than positives. We know, for example, that Warwick and Edward IV were not there (and probably Clarence too) We know that the Herbert brothers did not die at Edgcote. We know Stafford was not there (unless, of course, he was).

It is probably best to start with the conventional outline narrative discussed in Chapter 1. Under this narrative the campaign sees three actions, culminating in the battle at Edgcote. The first of these takes place just outside Northampton, when a force of riders from Pembroke's army tries to ambush the rebels' rearguard and is repulsed. There is then a skirmish the night before the battle, when Sir Henry Neville, Lord Latimer's son, is killed and then the actual fight on Danes Moor itself the following day.

Trying to get a clear timeline for these events is not easy. It is usually assumed that they happen close together, - almost on successive days. This would probably be based on the fact that Hall places the death of Sir Henry Neville on the day before the battle, and it is not very far from Northampton to Banbury. It is one of the key facts in the conventional battle narrative that Clapham marches from the area of Northampton to Edgcote in a day, arriving in time to determine the outcome of the battle. The distance is about 20 miles, and given the speed at which medieval armies could move this is entirely plausible.

There are some difficulties with this narrative. In the way it is described above it only exists in Hall. Polydore Vergil makes reference to a fight outside Northampton, and then also to one at Banbury, but not to the skirmish the night before. In fact, in Polydore Vergil it isn't a skirmish outside Northampton with a part of Pembroke's force. It is everyone. Pembroke and his full army pitch their tents at Northampton having found the Yorkshiremen camped there. The next day a battle is fought, and Pembroke is "quikly discomfytyd". No date is given for this battle.

What Hall and Poldore Vergil do agree on is that after the fighting outside Northampton a message was sent to Edward advising him of the reverse, to which he responded that Pembroke should not be down hearted and that he was on his way to help out, either that or he would send reinforcements. What we do not know, however, is exactly where Edward was when he received this message. The dates we have for his location based on letters he wrote and given under his seal in July are:

1st July - Fotheringhay (Coventry Leet Book)
5th July - Stamford (Coventry Leet Book)
9th July - Nottingham (Paston Letters)
10th July - Newark (Coventry Leet Book)
29th July - Nottingham (Coventry Leet Book)

It would appear that he was probably in the region of Nottingham, a round trip of 100 - 150 miles, depending on whether he was told of the defeat at Northampton from the location of the battle or from Banbury. That would imply at least two days for a man on horseback, or possibly even three, depending on whether regular remounts were available[1].

The Chroniclers are less precise about when and where the King was. Polydore Vergil claims the King was within 5 miles of Banbury on the same day, although he was not captured until after the executions of the Herberts, two days later. Hall implies he was further away than that, but was marching to the aid of Pembroke and Stafford.

There are clearly problems with the information we have about what is going on and where between the date of Warwick & Clarence's return to England on the 14/15th July and the capture of the King sometime after the 29th July, and whether or not the sequence of events happened as described.

So far in order to gain clarity of what happened on what day we have turned and looked to the Welsh poets. They are remarkably consistent about what happened from Monday the 24th July, the date of the battle, through to Thursday the 27th the date of the execution of William Herbert. What they do not give us is any account of feats of arms or tales of treachery on the field of combat in the days beforehand. Of course, absence of evidence is not evidence of absence, and stories of the two preceding fights might be missing because they were of such minor importance to the Welsh that they barely come to notice compared with the death of so important a man as the Earl of

---

[1] Sources for the speed of horses vary; the British Army would expect a mounted troop to travel a c5mph, with at least 5 hours break in every 24 (Field Service Pocket Book, 1914). The Pony Express could allegedly travel at 15mph or up to 25mph, changing horses every 10 miles.

Pembroke. That, or they might wish to overlook the unseemly defeat outside Northampton, and the unchivalrous killing of Sir Henry Neville as these might take the lustre off the nobility of the Welsh leaders.

However, it is not just the Welsh who overlook these earlier actions. De Wavrin, who provides other details, does not include the earlier fights either, unless the view is taken, as in Brooks[2], that the description he gives of the fight across the river takes place on one day, and the battle on Danes Moor the day after. Hearne's Fragment, Warkworth's Chronicle and Stow's Annales all do not report any other fighting, although all three of them record the death of Sir Henry Neville[3]. The Croyland Continuators record neither the earlier skirmishes, nor the deaths of any individuals.

The evidence for pre-battle encounters therefore comes from two sources, Polydore Vergil and Hall, and we have already established that Hall used Polydore Vergil's work, although it should be noted that only Hall has two pre-battle skirmishes. Hall appears to make more sense than Vergil and adds extra details that imply he had access to other sources, either written ones lost to us, or some word of mouth or family tradition. Whatever the source was, Stow does not appear to have been able to verify the information, because although he uses Hall, he only refers to the main fight at Edgcote itself.

All of which leads to the conclusion that most modern writers haven't looked too closely at all of the evidence, or simply have ignored the pieces that don't fit or appear to make a nonsense of the sequence of events. Hugh Bicheno, for example, has the skirmish outside Northampton on the 24th of July, and the battle at Edgcote two days later[4]. Ramsay likewise puts the battle at Danes Moor "within a day or two" of the fight at Northampton[5]. Both these writers either consciously ignore or simply overlook the assertion in Polydore Vergil, repeated in Hall, that messages passed between the royal army near Banbury or Northampton and the King in or around Nottingham. These would probably take two to three days or more and not the one or two that we have been allowed in these modern accounts. What is frustrating is that we do not have records of the letters sent either way, (if they were letters and not a verbal message given to a trusted servant) neither do we have the letters summoning Stafford and Pembroke which would provide greater certainty about where Edward was, and when he perceived he had a serious problem with the unrest in the North and the Earl of Warwick.

Why is this important? Other than a desperate desire to understand exactly what was going on the evidence points towards a different understanding of where the various components of the armies were and what the leaders' motivations were. One of the great mysteries of the Edgcote campaign is what was Edward playing at? His

---

[2] Brooks p256.
[3] William Worcestre also records the death of the son of Lord Latimer in casualties at the battle.
[4] Bicheno p123-4 As discussed above in Chapter 5, Bicheno uses the traditional date of the 26th for the main battle.
[5] Ramsay p341, although Ramsay places this skirmish at Daventry, not Northampton.

response to the rebellions in the North is dilatory to say the least. Following John Neville's suppression of the initial Redesdale rebellion which took place in late April/early May (according to the Beverley council records) there are further rebellions throughout the first half of 1469[6]. There is no doubt Edward knows about the problems, but he perambulates round the Home Counties and East Anglia, visiting pilgrimage sites and issuing the odd order to get war materials ready, before moving up to the Newark/Nottingham area where he seems to oscillate about for nearly three weeks.

During this time the Earl of Warwick is effectively re-running the 1460 Northampton Campaign, at almost exactly the same time of year. Leaving Calais shortly after the wedding of his daughter Isabel to George, Duke of Clarence, on the 11th July, he is in Canterbury around the 16th July, London on the 20th and then Northampton about a week later. The exact date of his arrival in Northampton isn't certain, but he was probably present for the execution of Sir Richard Herbert on Wednesday the 26th, and then for Sir William Herbert on Thursday the 27th. By way of comparison of the two campaigns, here are the time lines side by side[7]:

	1460 Campaign		1469 Campaign	
	Date	Days Elapsed	Date	Days Elapsed
Arrive Sandwich	27th June		13th July	
Arrive London	2nd July	5 days	20th July	7 days
Leave London	5th July	3 days	21st-22nd July	1-2 days
Arrive Northampton	10th July	5 days	26th-27th July	5-6 days

Warwick takes longer getting to London in 1469 as he spends two days in Canterbury collecting troops together. The dates for the leaving of London and arrival at Northampton in 1469 are slightly speculative. Warwick was in London long enough to negotiate a loan from the City[8], and then in Northampton for the executions, as discussed above. This is further evidence of the earlier date for the battle, because if it occurred two days later, on the 26th, then Warwick was very slow moving up the road to Northampton as the executions took place two-three days later, or the 28th & 29th on this time line. That means Warwick took eight days to cover ground he previously covered in five at a time when he was marching to make a rendezvous with his other forces, being those from the North.

Warwick's tardiness or otherwise seems to be immaterial, as Edward appears to be completely unaware of Warwick's location and intention, although as we can see from the "Paston Letters" dated 9th July he had his suspicions. He also appears not to

---

[6] Haigh "Where both the hosts" p16-31 concludes that there are three rebellions. See also K R Dockray's "Yorkshire Rebellions".
[7] Dates for 1460 are from Ingram p1. For 1469 combination of Haigh, "Where both the hosts", Bicheno, Schofield, Ramsay & Ross.
[8] Ross p130.

react - or at least move from the North East Midlands - when Warwick publishes a manifesto, calling upon people to attend him at Canterbury on the 16th July[9].

It might be, of course, that Edward is staying where he is in order to deal with the rebels should they march south, and is relying upon Pembroke & Stafford to deal with Warwick. If this is the case, he was seriously wrong footed, as the rebels appear to have gone past him without him being able to intervene, although as we don't know for certain where Edward was nor the route the rebels took we do not know if this was skill or good luck on behalf of the rebels.

It might be helpful here to look at the approximate distances the armies would have needed to travel to Northampton, which on the basis of the sources appears to be the intended initial destination of the various armies and not Banbury or Edgcote. The distances in the table below have been broken down to include the stopping off points Warwick is known to have used, and I have used distances from Doncaster via Leicester, not the Great North Road. For Pembroke I have assumed he left from Raglan, and Stafford from Bristol, the most northerly of the castles for which he was responsible. The distance from York is included should the reader prefer to believe that the rebels marched from further north.

	Canterbury	London	Northampton
Sandwich	15 miles		
Canterbury		57 miles	
London			67 miles (139 in total)
Doncaster			100 miles
Newark			65 miles
Nottingham			57 miles
Raglan			102 miles
Bristol			100 miles
York			134 miles

These numbers are a bit rough and ready, as they are based on walking distances on modern, non-motorway routes, but they do make something quite clear. All of Warwick's forces have much further to go to get to Northampton than Edward, as do Edward's allies. In fact, when contemplating the armies that might have been expected to fight in the East Midlands the one that should have got there first, based entirely on distance, was Edward. How many days these distances would have taken the armies to travel is open to a degree of conjecture. Armies could cover quite a distance when they were required to. Edward himself covered over 30 miles in a single day during

---
[9] The manifesto says "Caunterbury uppon Sonday next comyng", and is dated the 12th July. This was a Wednesday, so the Sunday would have been the 16th.

the Tewkesbury campaign[10], although 10 to 15 miles might be more reasonable, allowing for rest periods and encamping at the end of the day. Henry V's army in 1415 averaged just under 15 miles a day[11].

All of this makes it quite difficult to believe that Edward was in Nottingham on the 29th after he promised to come with support after the pre battle skirmish at Northampton. If there is enough time for a messenger to get to Edward in Nottingham and back then that fight takes place in the period 20th - 22nd July. This implies that Edward, who wrote a letter to Coventry on the 29th July from Nottingham (our only piece of dating evidence), actually did not move south to help out - other than potentially going from Newark to Nottingham - for at least a week. And during this time Warwick was able to get from London to Northampton and have his advance guard arrive at the battle, still finding time to borrow £1,000 from the London City Fathers on the way. Edward appears to be suffering from an incredible amount of inertia, complacency or just plain ignorance as to what is happening.

It is now time to look at the "battle" around Northampton in some detail and try to understand what the evidence is telling us. It is safe to say that Polydore Vergil's account is pretty much universally ignored by modern historians, - which is quite harsh, considering he is only one of two writers who discuss the fight. Ramsay sets the trend by referring to the action as a "reconnaissance in force", Bicheno prefers to refer to them as "Herbert's fore-riders", and Haigh as "mounted fore-runners"[12]. All of this relies upon Hall's account, where men from Pembroke's force, lead by Stafford and Sir Richard Herbert "go vewe and se the demeanor and nombre of the Northern men". This has normally been taken to imply that Pembroke and Stafford were at Banbury, and that his outriders had pressed up further north to locate the enemy, although Hall's account would seem to imply quite strongly that the reconnaissance party was sent out from "Cottishold", before the royal forces got to Banbury, the famous dispute over lodgings occurring after the skirmish at Northampton. It might be worth noting here that even with the small amount of detail contained in Hall's account, and rejecting what Polydore Vergil says, some writers choose to ignore what the Hall has written. Haigh goes as far as to say "it is unlikely to have been Sir Richard Herbert...or Devon in person".[13] It is difficult to see why Sir William Herbert would not have trusted his brother and colleague to provide him with reliable intelligence on the enemy's location and numbers. Edgcote, even more than many other medieval battles and campaigns, seems to suffer from a very selective use of evidence.

Hall's account is not entirely consistent with Polydore Vergil's version. As was noted above Polydore Vergil has the whole of Pembroke's army at Northampton, and defeated in a battle. The two accounts can be reconciled, for example, if what occurs

---

[10] Bicheno, p194.
[11] Curry, Appendix A p324-5.
[12] Ramsay p340, Bichno p123, Haigh "Where both the hosts" p32. Other writers ignore it completely, which is hardly surprising as the battle of Edgcote itself sometimes warrants only a few words.
[13] Haigh "Where both the hosts" p32.

is that the advance guard from Pembroke's army, or "Vaward" encounters the Northerner's army and is rebuffed, retiring with accounts that the royal army is outnumbered. It that was to be the case, the idea that it was lead by Sir Richard and Stafford becomes more plausible, and a force of "twoo thousande" men (as Hall puts it) out of c5,000 could easily be one of Pembroke's three "battles", or battlefield formations. Or even, perhaps, it was just a reconnaissance force, but one from an army camped near Northampton. As to the accuracy of the number of 2,000 in the force it is impossible to say, - as discussed in Chapter 3 none of the chronicler's numbers can be verified against each other or any other resource, and Hall is the only person to give numbers for this encounter.

The actual location of the "wood side" where the battle/skirmish is fought is unknown. As discussed in Chapter 4 Ramsay places it near Daventry, as have subsequent writers. One modern writer quoted in Haigh's "Where both the hosts fought" identifies the location as Plumpton Wood, outside Blakesley on Banbury Lane[14]. There is no particular reason to move the location from round the Northampton area. There are "wood sides" in numerous locations around Northampton, and if we take Hall at his word, - that the Northmen were "passyng towarde Northampton" - the wooded area is likely to be to the north of Northampton, in the direction of Market Harborough and Leicester. This, of course, is all speculative and does not accord with any other modern interpretation. The other implication of this interpretation is that Pembroke & Stafford moved even more quickly than it at first appears, if the whole of the army was at Northampton, and a sizeable force just to the north. The various sources we have refer to some of Pembroke's men being mounted, but not necessarily as cavalry. The forces that are rebuffed around Northampton are "well horsed Welshmen" according to Hall. Not cavalry, you will note, but "well horsed". English armies in particular[15], but armies in general, often gained strategic mobility by causing the foot to be mounted on lighter horses. Henry V took "mounted archers" to France with him in 1415[16], and the Beverley account book notes that their archers are sent to York on horseback.

What does seem to be the case, however, is that Pembroke was sufficiently concerned either with what had happened at or around Northampton, or the size of the rebel forces, that an urgent message was sent to the King, telling him the situation was much more serious than was at first thought.

Following the skirmish or battle around Northampton, the action next moves to Banbury, with the royal forces retreating down Banbury Lane, a retreat that could have taken one or two days, although likely to be a shorter period of time if they were concerned about pursuit from the rebels. This, again, is contrary to most modern interpretations, but does fit the evidence slightly better. If the army was approaching

---
[14] Quoted as being on p36 of R. P Jenkins "The Battle of Edgecote 26th July 1469". I have been unable to track down this publication and verify the reference.
[15] I am aware that Pembroke's force was made up of Welsh, not English.
[16] Curry p76.

Banbury and Edgcote from the North it does seem that it would be logical to camp the army in an open, defensible, position and then for the leaders to ride on to the nearest comfortable spot, rather then marching the army through Banbury and then returning.

This sequence of events also provides another explanation for the supposed falling out of the two commanders[17]. On arriving at Banbury it may well have been that Stafford had put Pembroke out of the place where he wanted to stay but that does beg a question. How did Pembroke, a nobleman from South Wales, and Stafford, a nobleman from the West Country know that there was a particularly lovely "damosell" at a certain inn in a small country town in the midlands[18]? Perhaps they had already been through Banbury on their way to Northampton, and were now retracing their steps.

What is equally possible is that following the retreat from Northampton, there were indeed "many great woordes and crakes", which perhaps included the poor performance of the advance guard when they ran into the rebels, which Pembroke's brother would have been able to describe, placing all of the blame on his colleague Stafford. Stafford getting ahead of the army on the retreat and pinching the best inn might just have been the last straw[19].

This dispute took place, according to Hall, on the day before the battle. None of the other chronicles that mention this incident (Hearne, Warkworth and Stow) give a date for it. Of the Welsh poets Guto'r Glyn refers explicitly to Devon fleeing, whilst the others refer only to treachery, all of which could be read as occurring during the battle as de Wavrin specifically says in his account. As already observed not all of the evidence in all of the accounts we have is mutually compatible. The tendency has been to accept the evidence that Ramsay accepted in Hall, and to overlook the pieces that he overlooked.

This may mean that the whole issue over lodgings is a complete fabrication, invented after the battle to save face for Pembroke, or to provide justification for Stafford retiring from the battle over a matter of honour, and not because he broke and fled with his men on hearing of the approach of rebel reinforcements. However, the frequency with which the story is repeated would indicate that there is probably a grain of truth in it or at least that there was a dispute between the commanders at Banbury. What this means is that there is sufficient ambiguity in the various accounts we have to pull apart the traditional timeline which goes, when applied to a battle date of the 24th July, like this:

---

[17] The following explanation is entirely conjectural, but no more so than some of the other interpretations that modern writers have come up with.

[18] Assuming, of course, that this is true and not just a bit of salacious gossip.

[19] Again, complete conjecture with no other evidence than human nature. Hearne's Fragment, Warkworth and Stow just refer to a difference over lodgings. The Welsh poets hardly mention it all, except to say that Stafford ran away.

Date	Day	Event
22nd July	Saturday	Skirmish at Northampton
23rd July	Sunday	Dispute at inn in Banbury
24th July	Monday	Battle of Edgcote

In practice it is more likely that there are several days either between the skirmish at Northampton and the dispute at Banbury, or between the latter and the battle, to allow for the messages to pass between the armies and their various overall commanders-in-chief. The fight at Northampton could very easily be as early as the 20th meaning the argument over the prostitute[20] in Banbury doesn't take place on the Sabbath. We could, for example, be looking at something more like this:

Date	Day	Event
20th July	Wednesday	Skirmish at Northampton
22nd July	Saturday	Dispute at inn in Banbury
24th July	Monday	Battle of Edgcote

Parsons Street Banbury today, home to two late medieval inns. Photograph © Graham Evans

---

[20] It is finally time to face facts about the "damousell". The oldest inns in Banbury which date back to medieval times are in Parsons Street. Parsons Street gained its name in 1410. Prior to that it was known as "Gropecunt Lane" in reference to the trade practiced there.

Why would there be a delay? The most obvious answer is given to us in Edward's reply to Pembroke, as reported in both Polydore Vergil and Hall: wait for me, I'm bringing reinforcements. As Hall put it "promisyng hym not alonely ayde in shorte tyme, but also he hymself in persone royall, would folowe hym with all his puyssance and power". Likewise in Polydore Vergil we are told for the rebels that "earle of Warweke, whan he had intelligence of thenemyes approche, sent with owt lingering unto the duke of Clarence, who was hard by with an army, that he wold bring his forces unto him, signyfying withall that the day of battayle was at hand".

What ever happened outside Northampton (if anything happened at all), whether it was a skirmish or a major clash, both sides now felt they needed to draw breath and wait for more forces before they committed to further action. What happened, as we will see, was that the rebels realised they would get their extra forces there first, and so moved down the Banbury Lane to fix Pembroke (and Stafford if he was there) in position.

The actual location of both Warwick's forces and Edward's now becomes more important. As we saw earlier, Warwick was in London on the 20th, leaving a day or two later, although it is possible that he pushed his advance guard ahead of him up the road to Northampton. Troops mounted on horses as a "flying column" could have been in Northampton and the area of Banbury in two to three days, and those from Nottingham sent by King Edward in a similar time frame. This means that time was of the essence for both sides, and the one that thought it would receive its reinforcements first would have to strike quickly and hard before the balance was tipped the other way.

In anticipation of the fight to come Pembroke had positioned his army in a strong defensible location, on a fairly flat hill top with easy access to water, and close enough to Banbury that the army commander could rest up in comfort. It is fairly safe to assume that having done this he deployed piquets at a distance from the camp to alert him should the rebels approach[21].

Meanwhile the rebels were based somewhere around Northampton, awaiting news from the Earl of Warwick of how close their reinforcements were. This news probably came sometime on the 23rd July, and the rebels headed down the Banbury Lane to engage Pembroke's forces. The first clash took place in the evening, as might be expected, as the rebel outriders encountered Pembroke's piquets. This lead to one of the more controversial actions of the campaign, which showed that there would be no holds barred.

The rebel scouts were lead by Sir Henry Neville, son of Lord Latimer, who was discussed in Chapter 6 as one of the candidates for "Robin of Redesdale", and during the encounter he seems to have pushed his luck a little bit.

---

[21] I have to confess that the account of the next few days and the battle is subject to some conjecture as we have little evidence as to exactly where everyone was and their motivations are not explicitly stated in any source. In my defence this applies to every other account written of the battle only no one else, as far as I can tell, is prepared to own up to using guess work.

Neville appears to have acted in a fool-hardy fashion and took his men very close to the royalist army's camp, where he performed "diuerse valiaunt feates of armes". In the heat of the moment he seems to have outstripped his support troops and was captured. What happened next had repercussions over the following days.

In order to understand it we need to look through the euphemisms in the writing. In this context "valiaunt feats of armes" means killing your opponents, it doesn't mean galloping up and down on a tournament field unhorsing fellow competitors. So what we have here is a fully, or well, armoured knight charging into the royalist piquets and camp guards and killing more than one or two of them. In his excitement he, as Hall puts it, "went so farre forward that he was taken and yelded". Therefore what has happened is that Neville, having charged into a group of the enemy and killing several of them, found he was isolated and surrounded. In an effort to save his own skin he then promptly surrendered in the expectation of clemency.

Why he thought he would be so treated, having slaughtered several of his opponents and in the middle of a war notorious for the execution of enemy leadership, is not explained, other than, presumably, he thought that he was operating under the usual chivalric rules that enabled fully armoured men to kill as many of the enemy as possible, then survive in the expectation of being ransomed. In keeping with what happened in other battles his expectation was disappointed, and he was "cruelly slain" by the Welshmen, presumably in retribution for their colleagues he had only so recently been cutting up, demonstrating once more that trying to surrender during a battle in the heat of the moment is a strategy fraught with danger.

What ever justification there may be for the killing of Sir Henry Neville, Hall tells us his men did not take it well, and the Welshmen were to reap the consequences the next day, when battle was joined in earnest.

When coming to discuss the battle the following day there are a number of difficulties. As will be no surprise the chronicle accounts that we have, whilst not exactly contradictory, are by no means complementary. Only de Wavrin and Hall give anything close to detailed descriptions of the battle. In fact some accounts say as much about the reason for the disagreement between Pembroke and Stafford as they do about the actual fighting.

To the narratives provided by de Wavrin and Hall we can add items of detail and colour from the Welsh poets. We have in Lewys Glyn Cothi's elegy for Thomas Vaughan the assertion that the rebels were on a hilltop near Banbury, as was discussed in Chapter 4. Elsewhere in the same poem we are told that Vaughan was wearing "white" armour, and that the Welsh were outnumbered. We also have a clear indication of the importance of archery at the battle, as Hywel Swrdwal in his elegy for William Herbert declares:

| Ni bo i berchen bwa | Let there not be a single goodnight |
| Racw'n swydd Iorc unnos dda | For the owner of a bow yonder in Yorkshire |

This is the first indication, chronologically, that the bow was a significant element in the battle. This is not the case for many battles in England in this period, Towton notwithstanding. The absence of archers in Pembroke's army, - or at least the implication that he has none, - appears firstly in Warkworth's chronicle, where he describes Pembroke's men as "the best in Wales", and Stafford as having archers from the West Country. Of course this does not mean that Pembroke had no archers but this point is made explicitly in Hearne's Fragment when it says "Lord Herbert came to Banbury with seven or eight thousand men without any Archers". As one might expect by now he is silent as to whether or not Stafford has any bowmen. Meanwhile the presence or otherwise of archers is not mentioned in de Wavrin's account, nor is it in Polydore Vergil.

It is Hall, inevitably, who gives us the fullest picture. Pembroke's men are "well furnished", whilst Stafford has 800 archers. When Stafford leaves Hall tells us that Pembroke was "vnpurueied of Archers".

The battle started early in the morning although there is no unanimity in the sources exactly how. From their camp near Thorpe Mandeville the rebels moved northwards in the valley to the west of Culworth, concealed from the royalist camp on Edgcote Lodge Hill. Presumably whilst this was happening Pembroke was putting on his armour in Banbury, kissing good bye to the "maid" at the inn and heading up to join his army.

The opening phase of the battle is in dispute. De Wavrin has both sides rushing towards the river between the two armies, on the eastern side of Danes Moor. Hall, however has the initial action as Pembroke's men being forced off their hilltop position by archery.

The easiest way to reconcile the two accounts is to postulate a probing attack by archers from the rebel army (see "Phase 1"map opposite). Perhaps in small numbers they advanced towards the foot of the hill and started to shoot at the royalists on the hill above them, aware that Stafford had left the army and headed back to the West Country with his archers, and that the Welsh were unable to shoot back.

When Pembroke arrived from Banbury and joined up with his army he took immediate action. Perceiving that the rebels were only few in number - assuming that the rest of the army was concealed behind the hill opposite - he gathered around him a group of mounted men and advanced down the hill to clear the rebels who were shooting at his army from the valley floor.

This tactic appears to have been successful. The rebel archers fell back towards the river crossing, drawing Pembroke's men forwards. As this was happening the rest of the rebel army moved up to provide support to their retiring forces, and attempted to hold the line of the river.

Pembroke could have been embarrassed at this point, as he had outstripped his infantry supports, who were still forming up. However, he held the river line in the face of increasing numbers of rebels and, as his infantry arrived, prevailed over the

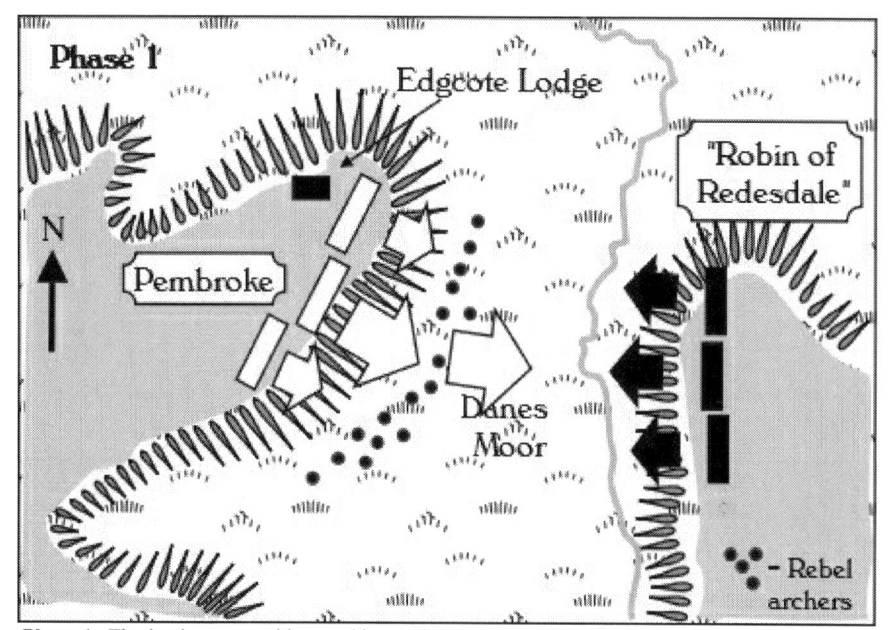

Phase 1: The battle opens with a probing archery attack, which Pembroke clears with a mounted counter-attack. Map © Graham Evans

enemy, who were forced to retreat. The fighting was hard and bloody and we are told that "many people were killed" (see "Phase 2" map overleaf).

There was then a lull in the fighting. For whatever reason Pembroke was unable or unwilling to follow up the rebels and inflict a complete victory. Perhaps, as is implied by the Welsh poet Lewis Glyn Cothi, Pembroke was still outnumbered and was standing on the defensive, waiting in vain for reinforcements from Edward or for Stafford to return[22].

In the event it was the rebels who received succour first. Two of Warwick's loyal knights arrived, presumably with their affinities, ahead of the main body. The two men were Sir William Parr, and Sir Geoffrey Gates. Gates was a long time supporter of Warwick, and held Calais for him as Marshal of Calais[23]. He would have been in his 60s at the time of the battle, and was a true hardened soldier. Sir William Parr's family seat was in Kendal[24], and as a supporter of the Yorkist faction in the north was allied

---

[22] Some accounts, including at the time of writing the Wikipedia entry, insist that Pembroke was expecting Stafford to rejoin him, Wikipedia even giving a time - 1pm - when news is received of Stafford's advance. This is complete invention. There is no evidence in any of the sources to suggest this to be the case.
[23] Coveney, Vol 1 A-H p31 Coveney curiously splits Gates' career over two entries, erroneously recording him as dying at Edgcote.
[24] Coveney Vol 3 S-Y p23.

to the Nevilles, or at least found it hard to say no to them. Although de Wavrin says that both knights came and joined the Northerners, it is possible that Parr was already there, being from a northern base, and made common cause with Gates, who had crossed over with Warwick from Calais.[25]

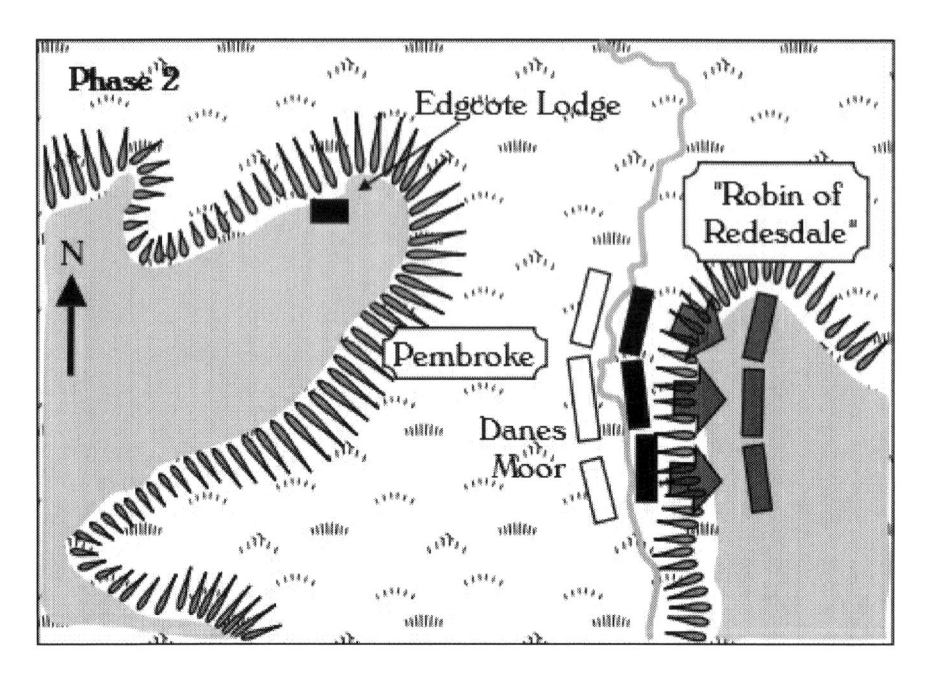

Phase 2: Pembroke drives the rebels' archers back to the river line, where he encounters the rest of the rebel army. The Welsh infantry eventually arrive to shore up his force, and the rebels are driven back to their opening position, leaving Pembroke holding the river line. Map © Graham Evans

Suitably reinforced the rebels returned to the attack (see "Phase 3" map opposite), and both armies set to it on Danes Moor. Perhaps it was at this time that Pembroke's brother, Sir Richard, performed his incredible feat of arms, described in Hall thus: "sir Richarde Herbert so valiauntly acquited hymself, that with his Polleaxe in his hand (as his enemies did afterward reporte) he twise by fine force passed through the bataill of his aduersaries, and without any mortall wounde returned".

This feat is a testimony not only to Sir Richard's martial prowess, but presumably also to the efficacy of late medieval suits of armour. Sir Richard's bravery and skill is recorded in Guto'r Glyn's elegy to his brother, when it says:

---

[25] Both Gates and Parr survived the cataclysm that was to befall Warwick, and became loyal followers of Edward. Parr acted as go-between in the 1470 rebellion, and joined Edward when he returned in 1471.

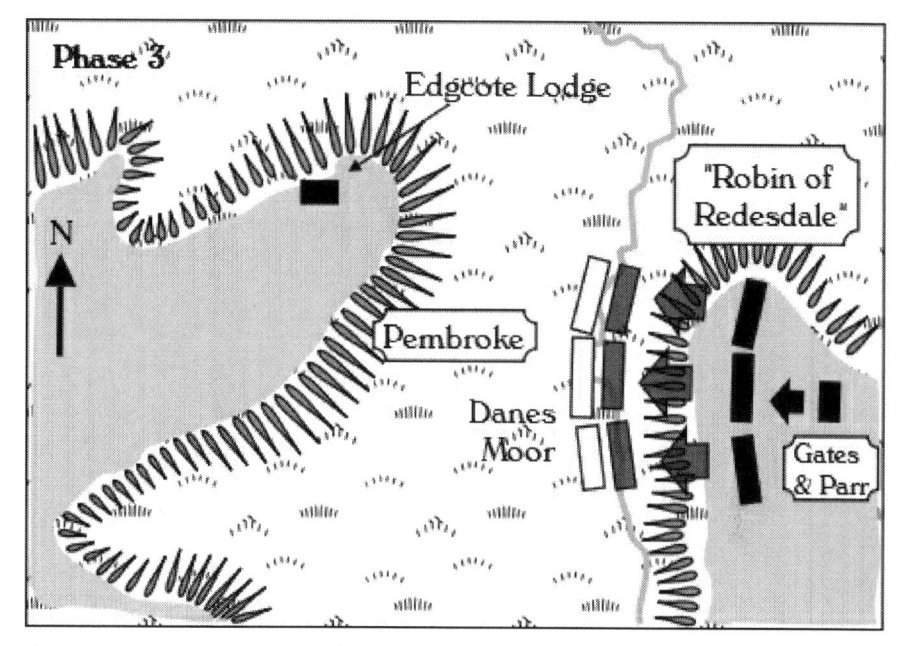

Phase 3: Reinforced by Sir William Parr and Sir Geoffrey Gates, the rebels counter attack. Map © Graham Evans

Marchog a las dduw Merchyr,	On Wednesday a knight was killed,
Mwy ei ladd no mil o wŷr:	killing him was a greater thing than a thousand of any other men:
Syr Rhisiart, ni syr Iesu	Sir Richard, Jesus won't be angry with him
Wrthaw er lladd North a'r llu.	for killing the Northerners and the host.

Note that the killing of the knight refers to his execution after the battle, - hence the reference to Wednesday.

This intervention by Sir Richard, despite the extra forces brought by the rebel knights Sir Geoffrey Gates and/or Sir William Parr, turned the battle in the favour of the Welsh. The rebels were starting to waver, when the final, decisive, intervention occurred.

De Wavrin says it was just a rumour, but Hall is adamant. Another wave of rebel reinforcements arrived, lead by John Clapham esquire.[26] Presumably the delay in their

---

[26] Just to show how a historian can mash up the sources to fit his own agenda, Oman, p187 says: "The King was only a few hours' march away; indeed, his vanguard under Sir Geoffrey Gates and Thomas Clapham actually reached the field, but both were old officers of Warwick, and instead of falling on the rebels' rear, proceeded to join them, and led the final attack on Pembroke's position" I have no idea how you can read any of the sources, even in isolation, and come up with this interpretation.

arrival was that the first wave consisted of mounted men, whilst Clapham's force was on foot. Or perhaps Clapham's men had taken a bit longer to assemble. Hall credits them with being only 500 strong, and not even a proper part of Warwick's army. They were "gathered of all the Rascal of the towne of Northampton and other villages about", and hastily fitted out with the Earl of Warwick's White Bear standards. It is just as easy to believe that Clapham had a core of Warwick's men with him, and used them to round up extra men, and hurry them the 20 miles down Banbury Lane.

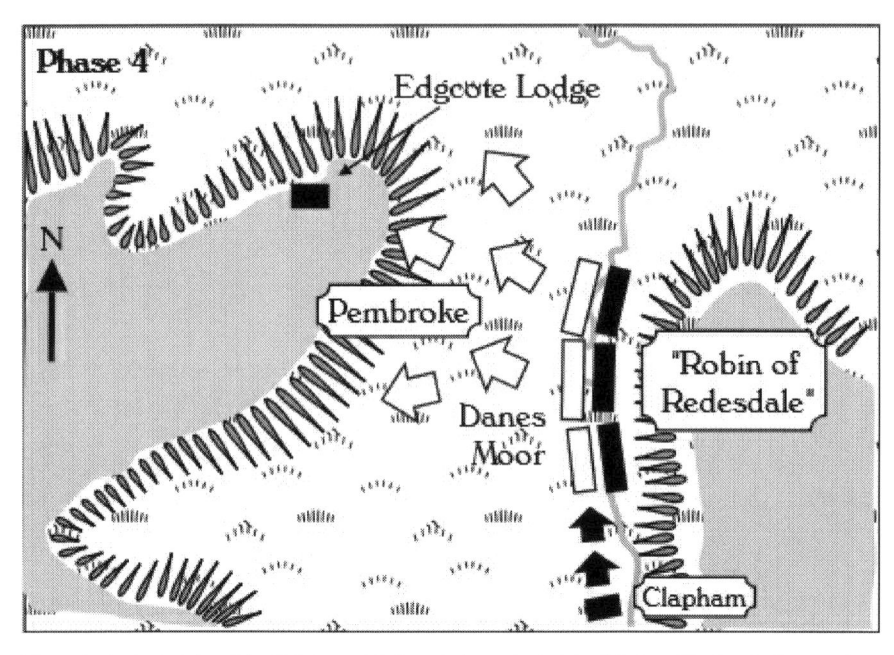

Phase 4: At the height of the fighting, with the rebels on the brink of defeat, Clapham's force arrives from Northampton, and Pembroke's army routs . Map © Graham Evans 2018

What ever the answer is, the result was conclusive. Coming round the side of the East Hill, where the rebels had originally revealed themselves to Pembroke's force, they fell on the flank of the Welshmen, and the army collapsed and fled[27] (see "Phase 4" map above). In view of the high death count amongst the Welsh nobility it is likely that they were forced to flee across a choke point, such as the crossing where Trafford Bridge now sits, rather than be dispersed across the Northamptonshire/Oxfordshire countryside. This implies that Clapham's men came around the southern side of the East Hill, - which is again consistent with coming down the Banbury Lane from Northampton.

---

[27] De Wavrin has it that it was Stamford/Stafford who fled with his men, on hearing of the arrival of rebel reinforcements.

The casualties amongst the Welsh leadership[28] may point towards a last desperate defence, as they tried to fall back in order, covering the retreat of their broken men. Both Sir William and Sir Richard Herbert were captured in the rout, as were other noblemen, - whether they yielded like the unfortunate Sir Henry Neville the evening before, or whether they were simply overwhelmed and beaten to the ground, bloodied and exhausted after a long day's fighting is not known. What is certain is that they did not mount up and abandon their men, and this was at some cost to the Herbert family. Not only were the two well known brothers captured, but two other Herbert brothers died at Edgcote[29]. The paeans to their bravery in the Welsh poems might well not be misplaced.

No confirmed grave pits for the fallen from this battle have been found, yet, in common with most of our battlefields from this period, so we do not know if the thousands of casualties in the chronicles - as many as 5,000 according to Hall - are close to being accurate. Whatever the number, the majority will be from the Welsh army, cut down as it tried to escape. Unlike other battlefields there is no "bloody meadow" or "battle dyke" to record for us still in the landscape where the slaughter took place, although "Warriors Wood" near Edgcote House might be a candidate.

What we do know is that it was an overwhelming victory for Warwick, - one of his most decisive, alongside Northampton, and he wasn't even there. And we can also see that Edward's tardiness had cost him a key supporter and a substantial armed force. What would the consequences of this mistake be?

---

[28] A list of the men killed, as given in the sources, is attached as an appendix to this chapter.
[29] I have tried to make sense of which Herbert was where, how many of them there were and their relationships to each other in attached appendix.

Appendix to "The Most Mighty Battlefield"
Welsh Casualties by Source

Warkworth's List	Stow's List	William Worcestre's List
Sere Rogere Vaghan, knyght	Sir Roger Vaughan knight	
Herry Organ sonne and heyre	Henry ap Morgan	
Thomas Aprossehere Vaghan, squyere	T ap Richard Vaughan Esquire	
William Harbarde of Breknoke, squyere	W. Herbert of Brecknocke Esquire	Willam Havard esq, Brecknock
Watkyn Thomas, sonne to Rogere Vaghan	Watkin Thomas sonne to Rog.Vaughan.	
Yvan ap Jhon of Merwyke	Inan ap Iohn ap Meridick	
Davy ap Jankyn of Lymmerke	Dany ap Iankin ap Limorik	
Harry Done ap Pikton	Harrisdon ap Pikton	Henry Don of Picton
John Done of Kydwelle	Iohn Done of Kidwelly	Henry Don of Kidwelly
Ryse ap Morgon ap Ulston	Rice ap Morgan ap Vlston	
Jankyn Perot ap Scottesburght	Iankin Perot ap Scotes Burg	
John Enead of Penbrokeschire	Iohn Euerard of Penbrokeshire	John Eynan of Pembrokeshire
Jhon Contour of Herforde.	Iohn Courtor of Hereford	
Thomas Harbarde was slayne at Brystow	Th Herbet was slain at Bristow	Thomas ap Roger esq brother of Ld Herbert
		Richard Herbert esq
		John ap Wyllem esq brother of Ld Herbert
		John (W)Ogan
		William Norman esq
		Thomas Barry
		Thomas Lewys esq, Chepstow
		Lewys Havard esq Brecknock
		Tomas Havard esq, Brecknock
		William Morgan of Brecknock
		Walter Morgan of Brecknock
		Walter Morgan of Brecknock (again)
		Henry Morgan of Brecknock
		Thomas Elys, gent
		Hoskyn Hervy of Kidwelly
		Meredith ap Gwyllym of Kidwelly
		Thomas Huntlee esq of Gwent
		Lord Herbert
		Sir Richard Herbert
		William Herbert, bastard brother of Lord Herbert in Bristol on Morrow of St James

Northerners Casualties by Source

Warkworth's List	Stow's List	William Worcestre's List
Sere Herry Latymere, sonne and heyre to the Lorde Latymere	Sir Henry Latimer, sonne and heire to the Lord Latimer	Son of Lord Latimer
Sere Rogere Pygot, knyghte	Sir Roger Pigot knight	
James Conya[r]s, sonne and heyre to Sere Jhon Conay[r]s, knyght	Iames Coniers, sonne and heire to sir Iohn Coniers knight	
Olivere Audley, squyere	Oliuer Audley Esquire	
Thomas Wakes, sonne and heyre to William Mallerye, squyere	Th. Wakes, sonne and heire to W. Mallory Esquire	
William Mallerye, squyere		
		Son of Lord Fitzhugh
		Son of Lord Dudley

The fates of the Herberts at and after Edgcote

	Earl of Pembroke Sir W Herbert	Sir Richard Herbert	Sir Henry Herbert	Sir Thomas/ Thomas ap Roger esq	William Herbert	John ap Wyllem
Relationship to Pembroke		Brother	Brother	Half brother	Bastard Brother	Brother
De Wavrin	Captured & executed at Northampton		Captured & executed at Northampton	Killed at Edgcote		
Guto'r Glyn	Executed on Thursday at Northampton	Executed on Wednesday at Northampton				
Hywel Swrdwal	Fought "with his brothers" executed Thursday	Executed Wednesday		"The Champion"		Proved himself a man
Brief Latin Chronicle	Captured & executed with two brothers					
Stow/ Warkworth	Beheaded Northampton	Beheaded Northampton		Slain at Bristol		
2nd Croyland	Captured & executed at Northampton					
Hearne's Fragment	Slain	Captured & executed at Northampton				
Polydore Vergil	Captured & executed					
Hall	Captured & executed at Banbury	Captured & executed at Banbury				
William Worcestre	Killed at Edgcote	Killed at Edgcote		Killed at Edgcote	Killed in Bristol on morrow of St James	Killed at Edgcote
Coventry Leet Book	Captured & executed at Northampton	Captured & executed at Northampton				

The genealogical records for the Herberts are not entirely clear. Pembroke's father was married twice and also had illegitimate children. The chroniclers may be in error in respect of some names. It might be hazarded that Wavrin's "Henry Herbert" is actually Sir Richard, and that Warkworth/Stow have mistaken Sir Thomas for William, the bastard brother. Note that Hywel Swrdwal has *three* Herbert brothers in addition to Pembroke at the battle (which is verified by William Worcestre), and that the Brief Latin Chronicle has two brothers executed with Pembroke. It is also worth noting that William of Worcestre lived in Bristol, so he is probably accurate about the death of Lord Herbert's "bastard brother", although it is possible he was a bastard son, and not a brother.

Chapter 8 - Retribution and Reckoning

There is no record that Warwick came to Banbury or Edgcote to survey the scene of his triumph. It might not, after all, have turned out as he had desired. True, Lord Pembroke, a man who he probably hated or at least resented for his influence with the King and the offices and land he had been given, had been delivered into his hands. Edward, however, had not. Nor had Edward conveniently been present, allowing for him to be killed on the battlefield and be replaced by his compliant brother.

Warwick had been down this path before, in 1460, and his actions although spread over several days mirror closely what he did then. Firstly he had enemies to deal with. The Battle of Northampton in July 1460 was immediately followed by a blood bath of on-battlefield executions. Once in Warwick's power the peers captured then were shown no mercy, with the Duke of Buckingham, Earl of Shrewsbury, Lord Egremont and Viscount Beaumont all being killed. Warwick was not a forgiving man.

Warwick was not present at Edgcote so we do not know if the men who died were killed in combat or executed on capture. The sources are silent on any on-battlefield executions, so it is most likely that the cold blooded removal of enemies and rivals did not take place on the day. We do know that the two Herbert brothers were taken prisoner and dragged to Northampton, where Warwick was waiting[1]. The leader of the rebels, - Willoughby in de Wavrin, and Sir John Conyers in Hall, - brought the unfortunate Welshmen forwards, whereupon Sir William started to plead for his brother's life, on a "take me, not him" basis. It was then that the killing of Sir Henry Neville came back to haunt them. According to Hall, Conyers, backed up by Clapham, (who, of course, was not present when Sir Henry was killed) brought the death of Lord Latimer's son to Warwick's attention, and he had no compunction about ordering their deaths. It is to be seriously doubted that Warwick would have allowed them to live regardless of the killing of Sir Henry, but it cannot be doubted that Warwick was prepared to make the most of the whole affair, having Sir Richard beheaded on the Wednesday, and his older brother the day after[2]. Local tradition has it that the executions took place at the Eleanor Cross. This would certainly have re-emphasised the link with Warwick's triumph over another King nine years earlier, as the Cross stands on the corner of the 1460 battlefield.

The other royalist army leader didn't fare any better, despite leaving the Banbury area before the fighting. As Guto'r Glyn remarked:

| Arglwydd difwynswydd Defnsir | The lord of Devon, his service was worthless, |
| A ffoes – ni chafas oes hir | fled – he didn't live long! |

---
[1] The one thing that all the sources agree on is that the Herbert brothers were executed in Northampton, except for Hall, who places the executions at Banbury.

[2] De Wavrin declares that Warwick turned them over to the people of Northampton, who stoned them to death, or "miserably put them to death" depending on the version of the text used.

The Coventry Leet Book rather cold-bloodedly puts it, in best official notation;

"Item Lord Southwick was taken at Bridgewater and there beheaded."

Warkworth, Hearne's Fragment and Hall all record the incident in mostly the same words, except to say that he was taken by "the Commons", Hall adding that it was on King Edward's orders, although this seems out of character for a man as forgiving as Edward, especially at a time when he was otherwise quite busy. The undertones of lynching in this short episode would almost predispose the reader towards something less clinical than a beheading, and perhaps de Wavrin's account of a stoning at Northampton refers instead to the demise of Stafford.

Having indulged himself in bloody retribution, Warwick was not quite finished. Unlike 1460 the battle had not lead to the immediate capture of the reigning monarch on the battlefield, nor had it provided him with an opportunity to do away with those of Edward's councillors he most hated. The chroniclers usually report the disposing of Edward's favourites before going on to discuss what Warwick did about Edward but the sequence of events is different.

What was most important immediately after the battle was where was Edward, and what was to be done with him? Warwick clearly didn't have an instant answer. We know that Edward was in Nottingham on the 29th July, from the letter in the Coventry Leet Book, and we have evidence, which will be discussed later, of him being in Coventry on the 2nd August. The journey between the two cities is a matter of 50 miles, something Edward could have done in two days if he had desired.

The letter from Edward to Coventry is sometimes seen as evidence that Edward was in ignorance of the outcome of the battle five days earlier. For this to be the case it would mean that the post-battle security operation carried out by Warwick's forces was incredibly effective, - either that or the Welsh army was so busy trying to save its own collective skin that no one thought to ride to the King to bring him the bad news. That is more plausible if the battle was fought on the 26th and not the 24th as was established earlier. However, what if we were to look at the letter in the light of the idea that Edward knew about the defeat, and it was written during the period which Hall describes thus: "Herauldes spared no horseflesh in riding betwene the kyng and the erle, nor in retornynge from the Erle to the kynge: the kynge conceyuinge a certayne hope of peace in his awne imagination". Both Polydore Vergil and Hall describe a period where negotiations are clearly taking place between Edward and Warwick, with Warwick trying to convince the King that his only hope is to come to Warwick at a place of his choosing, and reach some sort of agreement.

Edward's Coventry letter seems to be saying thank you for the city's support (presumably the 82 archers got to him) and their concern for his well being and safety, and assuring them of his goodwill for the future. It could be read that Edward is sounding the city out as a safe place to go, possibly to meet up with Warwick.

It is generally overlooked that both Hall and Polydore Vergil claim that Edward was close to the battle, having marched towards Pembroke & Stafford. This could simply mean he moved from Newark to Nottingham. If so, it doesn't fit with Polydore Vergil's claim that he was within 5 miles of Banbury on the evening of the battle, nor his message to Pembroke on hearing of the defeat at Northampton "promisyng hym not alonely ayde in shorte tyme, but also he hymself in persone royall, would folowe hym with all his puyssance and power".

What does fit in with these messages and the time available is the idea that Edward had marched south of Nottingham and that he was in the region of Banbury on the 24th or 25th. On learning of the defeat of his main allies, and getting news that Warwick had unified his forces, he then fell back towards Nottingham, where Warwick's Heralds first approached him. After several days of negotiations Edward then wrote to Coventry, and confident that he would be safe, headed south to the city.

The exact location of Edward's capture as well as the circumstances, are also a matter of some debate. The geographic clues are not always clear, and do not tie in to one location. Part of the confusion arises as there are three villages with similar names in the Midlands that could do service for the location; Olney in Buckinghamshire, the now deserted village of Onley near Barby in Warwickshire, and Honiley, also in Warwickshire.

De Wavrin, who provides the most detailed and graphic account of the King's capture which we will get to later, does not tell us where the King was, only that he was taken to the Earl of Warwick and the Duke of Clarence, somewhere between Warwick (the place) and Coventry, and that he was lodging near to Warwick. This probably refers to Warwick the person, not the place, although both were fairly close to each other at this time. Warkworth says it was in a village "bysyde Northampton", which might imply Olney although with it being 12 miles to Olney, 18 miles to Onley and 38 miles to Honiley it is only "beside Northampton" relative to the other two.

The Third Croyland Continuator favours a Warwickshire Onley/Honiley, saying the location was "a certain village near Coventry", but at 15 miles, Onley isn't exactly close although Honiley at 10 miles might be considered so. More geographical inexactitude comes from Hall, who tells us the location was "Wolney. iiij. myle from Warwycke". Onley is 18 miles, and Olney over 40, so it is stretching the point in any event for either of them. Honiley, however, is about 7 miles, and this distance is consistent with Hall describing Edgcote as being 3 miles from Banbury when it is closer to 6. Finally, Stow goes for "Ulnay, a village before Northampton", probably drawing on Warkworth.

The balance of the evidence would point towards Honiley as Ramsay decided at the end of the 19th century[3]. At the time Honiley Manor was held by the Mountford family[4], with the current incumbent being Sir Simon. Sir Simon was certainly an Edward loyalist,

---

[3] Ramsay p343.
[4] A History of the County of Warwick: Volume 3, Barlichway Hundred. Honiley p120-123.

and went into exile with him in 1470, before returning and fighting for him at Barnet and Tewkesbury[5].

Bearing in mind what follows it is most likely that the location was nearer to Coventry, and not South of Northampton, on the way to London. There is a difference of opinion as to whether Edward had an army with him, as he came south (Hall says that he had "a great armye, and euer as he wente forwarde, his company increased") or whether he was friendless (as Croyland Continuator number two puts it "those who had hitherto remained firm in their allegiance to him, now became greatly alarmed, and basely deserting him by thousands, clandestinely took to flight"). Perhaps the Croyland Chronicle has it the most correct, with Edward starting accompanied by a large army, which steadily disintegrates as it heads towards the combined army of Warwick and Clarence.

As the "armies" approached each other, Warwick proved himself to be the more wily strategist. He was aware of Edward's movements and actions through more effective scouting, or through the use of "espials" as Hall and Polydore Vergil put it. He was aware, therefore, when Edward stopped for the night at Honiley with a relatively weak guard.

If Edward had been heading to see Warwick in the expectation that some form of negotiation was to take place, - which would seem to be the case, otherwise why would he risk being so close to the most powerful nobleman in England - he was soon to be disabused of that notion. In Hall and Polydore Vergil the King's camp is taken by surprise by a small elite group of soldiers selected by Warwick, who killed the guards in the dead of night and dragged the King from his bed.

Hall and Polydore Vergil are the only chroniclers who describe the King's capture in this way. Warkworth, Stow and the Croyland Chronicle all assign a role to George Neville, the Archbishop of York.

The fullest version, however, is contained in de Wavrin's account, and is generally followed by most historians[6]. No one is prepared to accept the Polydore Vergil/Hall version, although it does seem to fit well with Warwick's character.

De Wavrin's story has a wealth of detail and the ring of truth. It also, very rarely for all of our chronicles covering this campaign, contains some reported speech. The story goes like this.

Edward, having been made aware of the deaths of the Herbert brothers, rides to meet his brother and cousin, making noises that he is going to avenge himself on his perfidious brother. He seems not to be accompanied by an army. Perhaps, as has been suggested above, it was part of the deal the heralds had made when they negotiated the terms under which Warwick and Edward would meet. Perhaps Edward was sufficiently reassured by the response from his "Trusty and wel-belouyd...Cite of Couentre" that he expected to be safe within the castle or city walls, or maybe his supporters had melted away, or as Hall puts it "the kynge conceyuinge a certayne hope

---
[5] Coveney, T, Vol 3 S-Y p20.
[6] Which is ironic, as his account of the battle is often overlooked.

of peace in his awne imagination, toke bothe lesse hede to him selfe, and also lesse fered the outward atteptes of his enemyes, thinkyng and trustynge truely that all thynges were at a good poynt and should be well pacified".

As it was, Edward might have had a suspicion that things weren't going to plan, as he got within sight of Coventry. The harbingers of the royal party - the officers of the Royal Household or the army who travelled ahead to identify and allocate lodgings - found the inn they were intending to use in Coventry not available, and the Northern rebels in occupation of the city. The harbingers left in a hurry, barely escaping with their lives. As it was probably late in the day, Edward and his lightly armed party (de Wavrin says unarmed) moved to the village of Honiley as discussed above, and took lodgings with a trusted supporter.

This was what Warwick had been waiting for, on the advice of his brother, the Archbishop of York. At around midnight George Neville, with a party of soldiers, hammered on the door of Honiley Manor, seeking admittance. Once inside, he demanded of the King's bodyguards that he must speak to the King. Edward, being Edward, seems to have taken this in his stride, and responded that he had retired for the night, and would see him in the morning. The Archbishop was not in a position to take no for an answer. He had already thrown his lot in with the rebels and would have to answer to his brother if he failed in his mission. He sent the message again, saying it was essential that he speak to the King. Edward gave in, and allowed him in to his bedchamber, where he was already in bed.

On entering the chamber, Neville said to the King "Sire, get up!". Still trusting he could face down any threat, Edward remarked that he had not had any rest as yet, and begged to be excused.

This scene is portrayed in an illustration in the de Wavrin manuscript that shows the Archbishop in the King's chamber[7]. How reliable a representation of the event it is, is difficult to say. Edward is in bed wearing a nightcap, with his armour, in the glorious way that medieval illustrations usually ignore perspective, arrayed on the wall or floor next to him. The figure of Edward looks curiously thin and frail for a man reputed to be of considerably size and stature. Contrary to the way the event appears in the text the Archbishop is shown kneeling next to his King, almost begging him to get out of bed, - although he does have two fully armoured men accompanying him.

But Archbishop Neville[8] was not to be denied, and said, "You have to get up and come to my brother of Warwick, and no objection is possible". In more modern times he might have added "Resistance is Futile". It was only then that Edward finally admitted that he had been outmanouevred, and fearing the worse, - who knows, perhaps by this time his room was full of soldiers - he got dressed, and went with the Archbishop to meet with the Earl of Warwick, and his own faithless brother, George, Duke of Clarence.

---

[7] Hicks, "The Wars of the Roses" p40.
[8] "as the false and disloyal man that he was" - de Wavrin.

It is normally said that the meeting took place between Warwick and Coventry, perhaps Kenilworth, which is indeed about half way between the two, and only four or five miles from Honiley. The illustration discussed above also shows the King being presented to Warwick and Clarence in their camp. The King is fully armoured in this picture, with the Crown on his head, whilst Warwick and Clarence have an army complete with artillery. The army seems to be encamped outside a village or town. Again, how useful a guide it is to what happened it is difficult to say.

After being delivered to the two traitors it is said that Edward was taken immediately to Warwick Castle, but there is evidence that he was in Coventry too, as was mentioned above. According to a note in the 1874 edition of the Paston Letters[9] he signed against the Privy Seal in Coventry on the 2nd August. He then signed again at Warwick, on the 9th, 12th and 13th August.

Whilst this was going on, and the King was incarcerated, Warwick continued the hunt for his enemies at court. Edward had tried to hide his in-laws away, but Lord Rivers and his son, Sir John Woodville (the King's father-in-law and brother-in-law respectively) were captured on the Welsh borders, either at Chepstow or in the Forest of Dean. The Forest of Dean is favoured by Warkworth, Hall and Stow, although it would appear from some internal evidence that Stow had access to both Hall and Warkworth, so this could all be from a single source.

The main thing that is certain about Lord Rivers and Sir John is that they are executed by beheading. The majority of chroniclers place these executions in Northampton[10]. In the case of Hearne's Fragment and Hall they are taken by the "Northmen", and in Hall's version accompanied by men of Northamptonshire, once they have elected their own "Robin of Riddesdale". Hall also has them finding Rivers at the family seat in Grafton Regis with his son.

However, our most reliable piece of evidence is our anonymous clerk maintaining the Mayor's records in the Coventry Leet Book who, again in a matter of fact way, records:

"Item On Aug. 12 in the same year Lord Rivers then Treasurer of England was beheaded at Gosford Green, and Lord John Woodville, his son, likewise; they had been taken at Chepstow."

As Gosford Green[11] is just outside Coventry it seems unlikely that a city official would make such an elementary error. Especially as the entry contains such a specific date and is a contemporary record. The use of a Warwickshire location for the

---

[9] Paston Letters, vol ii, p xlix, note 2.
[10] Warkworth, Hearne's Fragment, Hall & Stow.
[11] Gosford Green is a place redolent with Yorkist/Lancastrian history. It is at Gosford Green that Richard II commanded Henry Bolingbroke and Thomas Mowbray to meet to settle their duel over accusations of treason. Both were exiled before the duel could take place. The symbolism would not have been lost on Warwick. "A History of Warwickshire" (1889) by Samuel Timmins, p238.

executions is supported by the "Brief Latin Chronicle" that confirms the date of the 12th August, only moving the actual deed just down the road slightly to Kenilworth.

What this does is place the executions, probably overseen by Warwick, close to him and the King. It is at this time, as we have already seen, that Edward is using the Privy Seal in Coventry and Warwick, under the Earl's direction. It may be no coincidence that the date of two of the uses the 12th & 13th, are at the time of the executions of Edward's father-in-law and brother-in-law, just up the road, outside Coventry. Maybe Warwick needed something to show his cousin to prove that he was not fooling about, and that, although he was King, he had no one else to turn to.

Chapter 9 - Aftermath and Afterthoughts

It is universally agreed that after a week or so of incarceration in the Midlands Edward was moved north, to Warwick's stronghold of Middleham or to York. There Warwick tried to use Edward as a puppet, but found him considerably less tractable than Henry VI had been following his capture at the Battle of Northampton.

It is not the intention here to go through the subsequent events in detail, but to consider what the campaign and battle meant to the main players involved and to the Kingdom as a whole.

Warwick's inability to build a solid administration in the face of Edward's bloody mindedness not to co-operate meant that his gamble to run the country through a Yorkist proxy had failed. Edward called his bluff in terms of his willingness to put an anointed King to death, and Warwick seems to have been unable to convey a further message to the populace at large that he should be allowed to run the country. The backbone of his campaign had been the need to remove the King's evil councillors. Having done so the populace seems to have thought that it was job done, and the King could now get on with running the country with more suitable advisors. This was contrary to what Warwick desired, which was to run the country but with a suitable King to provide legitimacy.

Whether Warwick realised it immediately or not his bolt with this branch of the Plantagenets was shot. If he was to thrive and grow his power even more then he needed another strategy. Typically for Warwick he did try the Northern Rebellion trick again, in 1470, ending in the "Battle" of Losecote Field. This resulted in victory for Edward and left Warwick and Clarence fleeing to the continent. It took Warwick's alliance with Margaret of Anjou and the marriage of Edward of Westminster, Henry VI's son, to Anne Neville, to convince Clarence that he had backed the wrong horse.

Warwick seemed to have chosen the correct strategy when he engineered the readeption of Henry VI, forcing Edward to flee. Edward's return the following year saw him reconciled with Clarence[1] and conduct the two campaigns that saw the death of Warwick at the Battle of Barnet on the 14th April 1471 and then that of Edward of Westminster at Tewkesbury on the 4th May the same year. Edward had gone from being a prisoner in the hands of an over-mighty subject to undisputed monarch with all his major rivals dead in less than two years.

The significance of Edgcote and the associated campaign is that it represents the point of no return for Warwick, and it shows him as an over-ambitious man who had run out of ideas or common sense. Once he realised he was unable to control Edward when he was, in theory, completely powerless, he was inevitably on the road to an alliance with the Lancastrians. Edward was a very forgiving man, but Warwick had overstepped the mark.

---

[1] Clarence, of course, didn't learn and turned on his brother again, leading to his private execution in 1478 for treason. Or probably more likely for trying his big brother's patience just once too often.

That is why it is important to understand what is going on in these few short months. Hindsight is always a problem when looking at history, but Warwick's career over these months is a car crash in slow motion. There are points when he could have made different decisions and pulled out of the fateful events, when he could, perhaps, have reconciled himself to the fact that whatever Edward was doing in flexing his muscles as a man growing into the job of King, he, Warwick, was still a very wealthy man, with a lot of influence and the ability to provide good lordship.

The 1469 Campaign has many parallels with that of 1460, and it ends in a similar way, with an overwhelming victory, the capture of a King and the execution of political rivals. What it doesn't have is a submissive, weak-minded monarch as the prisoner. There is a case for believing that some of the plan went off at half-cock. There is a lot we do not know, and the exact intentions of the plotters aren't committed to paper anywhere, except in the Manifesto published by Warwick and Clarence. The preceding chapters have analysed what we have as evidence in a lot of detail and the reader can follow the line of reasoning and draw their own conclusions as to whether the battle was the result of a chance encounter or was deliberately engineered to be when and where it was. One writer is certain the battle was not intended by either side, and that Warwick wanted Edward present so he could die in battle[2]. Against a man such as Edward this was a high risk strategy. He had already fought in three battles so far in his young life and been on the winning side in all of them, - a record he was to keep over the rest of his military career as well.

It is clear from what we have looked at here that as a historical event the 1469 campaign has not been as well served by historians as it could have been. The general reluctance of many historians to deal in detail with military events with the same level of diligence as they might spend on diplomatic negotiations or the trading rights of the Hanseatic League means we have the regular repetition of incorrect dates for significant events and a misunderstanding of who was where and why. The willingness to accept that armies larger than the population of London marched and fought in a small area of the East Midlands should give us all pause for thought.

Other than the impact on the major figures in the campaign what was the impact on the Kingdom as a whole? Taken with the events of 1471, which saw the final fall of the Earl of Warwick, the fallout was considerable.

The affect on Wales requires a full and proper study, beyond the scope of this work. It is unbelievable that the only dedicated work that even touches on the subject is over 100 years old[3]. Even this does not cover in detail the appalling effect the losses of so many Welsh leaders had. You only have to turn to the limited number of poems reprinted here to see how deeply the Welsh psyche was scarred by these events, and how it was seen as a national tragedy. In practical administrative terms Wales had been divided between Pembroke and Warwick,[4] with Pembroke holding the lion's share. In two years' time both of them would be gone, along with many what would now be

---

[2] Bicheno p111 & p122.

[3] H T Evans "Wales and the Wars of the Roses" was published originally in 1915.

[4] Bicheno has a very good map showing the distribution of estates just before the Edgcote campaign on p67.

termed "community leaders". Chaos came to the Principality with men looking for revenge. As Hywel Swrdwal put it:

| Edward wyn, dyred unwaith | Blessed Edward, come sometime |
| I Gymru i enynnu'n iaith. | to Wales to ignite our nation. |

He then goes on to demand all forms of vengence on the "bastard sons of Horsa and Hengist". Guto'r Glyn is even more despairing of what has happened and what the future holds:

Ef a'm llas, mi a'm nasiwn,	I was killed, I and my nation too,
Yr awr y llas yr iarll hwn,	the moment that this earl was killed,
Cymro oedd yn ffrwyno Ffrainc,	a Welshman who used to bridle France
Camreol Cymry ieuainc.	and the misrule of young Welshmen.
Ofn i bawb tra fu 'n y byd,	He inspired fear in all while he was in the world,
Yn iach ofn oni chyfyd!	farewell to fear now unless he comes back to life!
Ymgyrchu i Gymru a gân',	They will be able to march on Wales now,
Ymsaethu 'm Mhowys weithian.	to make arrow-play in Powys.
Doed aliwns, nis didolir,	Let aliens come, they won't be driven away,
O dôn', pwy a'u lludd i dir?	if they do come, who will stop them landing?

Not only did lawlessness beckon in Wales. Neville's fall left a vacuum in the North, ready to be filled by the Lancastrian leaning Percys. Edward's solution was to throw the problem to his remaining trustworthy brother, Richard of Gloucester. It was out of the crisis of 1469-71 that the power-base Richard was to develop grew, with future consequences for Edward's young heirs.

The shadow cast by Edgcote was long indeed.

Appendix - Primary Sources

This appendix contains extracts from all of the Primary Sources used in the preparation of this book, where these are available free of copyright. These have been taken directly from the original publication of the works, without any changes to update the spelling or grammar in an effort to make them accessible to a modern audience. It is assumed that if the reader has bought a book of this type and made it this far he or she will not be put off by some late medieval or early renaissance spelling.

Where the works are not in English they have been translated by me, or where indicated, a professional translator. The originals have normally been included as well as the translations so that the reader can see what was written and what I understand the text to mean.

I am delighted to include new translations of the works of several Welsh poets prepared by Ann Parry Owen from the University of Wales Centre for Advanced Welsh & Celtic Studies with the assistance of Jenny Day. Their enthusiasm for these works is inspiring. Whilst quotations from these poems occasionally appear in works on the battle, the full poems deserve more attention and notice. They are still incredibly vibrant over 500 years later, filled with wonderful language and imagery and driven by burning passion.

List of Sources

Report on the Manuscripts of the Corporation of Beverley	89
Warwick's Manifesto	90
The Coventry Leet Book or Mayor's Register	93
The Paston Letters 1422-1509 Volume 5	98
Marwnad Wiliam Herbert o Raglan, iarll cyntaf Penfro	99
Marwnad Tomas ap Syr Rhosier Fychan	102
Marwnad Wiliam Herbert	105
Recueil des croniques et anchiennes istories de la Grant Bretaigne - Jean de Wavrin	108
A Brief Latin Chronicle	115
Warkworth's Chronicle of the First Thirteen Years of the Reign of King Edward the Fourth	117
Ingulph's Chronicle of the Abbey of Croyland	119
Hearne's Fragment	123
Three books of Polydore Vergil's English History, comprising the reigns of Henry VI, Edward IV, and Richard III	125
The Union of the Two Noble and Illustre Famelies of Lancastre & Yorke ("Hall's Chronicle")	129
Annales, or a Generale Chronicle of England from Brute until the present yeare of Christ 1580	134
The Annales of England	135

Report on the Manuscripts of the Corporation of Beverley

Historical Manuscripts Commission, HMSO 1900

Extract from page 144

f. 161. 23 Feb. 9 Edw. IV. Letters testimonial under the common seal to John Maikewhate, tailor, " ad testificandum innocentiam suam de causando mortem Ing. Lepton, ballivi libertatis Archiepiscopi."

f. 161 h, 1469. " Sagittarii conducti pro communitate ad equitandum cum Domino Northumbriae pro repressione Hob. De Redesdale et aliorum inimicorun Domini Regis in crastino S. Marci ix° E. IV., existentium in negotio praedicto per ix dies." 6 at 6s. each, and 3s. 4:d. " in regardo " to the Bailiff, with other expenses 10d.

18 June. "Armati et sagittarii " for 3 days.

f. 162 h. Money borrowed to pay them.

Translation

f. 161. 23 Feb. 9 Edw. IV. Letters testimonial under the common seal to John Maikewhate, tailor, to prove their innocence in causing the death of Ing. Lepton, bailiffs of the liberty of the Archbishop.

f. 161 h, 1469. Archers sent from the community on horseback to the Lord Northumberland for the suppression of Hob. of Redesdale and other enemies of the Lord King on the morrow of S. Mark[1] ix° E. IV., taking part in the above business for nine days

18 June "Weapons and bowmen" for 3 days

f. 162 h. Money borrowed to pay them.

[End of Extract]

---

[1] St Mark's Day is the 25th April.

Warwick's Manifesto

Taken from "Warkworth's Chronicle of the First Thirteen Years of the Reign of King Edward the Fourth" ed J O Halliwell, Camden Society 1839

Extract from pages 46 - 49

The duc of Clarance, th'archebisshoppe of Vorke, and th'erle of Warwyk.

    Right trusty and welbelovid, we grete you welle. And welle ye witte that the Kyng oure soveregne lordys true subgettes of diverse partyes of this his realme of Engelond have delivered to us certeyn billis of Articles, whiche we suppose that ye have in thoos parties, rememberynge in the same the disceyvabille covetous rule and gydynge of certeyne ceducious persones; that is to say, the Lord Ryvers, the Duchesse of Bedford his wyf, Ser William Herbert, Erle of Penbroke, Humfrey Stafford, Erle of Devenshire, the Lordis Scalis and Audeley, Ser John Wydevile, and his brethern, Ser John Fogge, and other of theyre myschevous rule opinion and assent, wheche have caused oure seid sovereyn Lord and his seid realme to falle in grete poverte of myserie, disturbynge the mynystracion of the lawes, only entendyng to thaire owen promocion and enrichyng. The seid trewe subgettis with pitevous lamentacion callyng uppon us and other lordes to be meanes to oure seid sovereyne Lord for a remedy and reformacion; werfore we, thenkyng the peticioun comprised in the seid articles resonabyll and profitable for the honoure and profite of oure seid sovereyn Lord and the comune welle of alle this his realme, fully purposed with other lordis to shewe the same to his good grace, desiryng and pray you to dispose and arredie you to accompayneye us thedir, with as many persones defensabyly arrayede as y can make, lettyng you wete that by Goddis grace we entende to be at Caunterbury uppon Sonday next comyng.
    Wretyn undre oure signettis and signe manuell the xijth day of Juyll, A° 1469[1].

In three the next articles undrewretin are comprisid and specified the occasions and verry causes of the grete inconveniencis and mischeves that fall in this lond in the dayes of Kyng Edward the ij^{de}, Kyng Ric the ij^{de}, and Kyng Henry the vith, to the distruccion of them, And to the gret hurt and empoverysshyng of this lond.

    First, where the seid Kynges estraingid the gret lordis of thayre blood from thaire secrete Councelle, And not avised by them; And takyng abowte them other not of thaire blood, and enclynyng only to theire counselle, rule and advise, the wheche persones take not respect ne consideracion to the wele of the seid princes, ne to the comonwele of this lond, but only to theire singuler lucour and enrichyng of themself and theire bloode, as welle in theire greet possessions as in goodis; by the wheche the

---

[1] 12th July 1469 was a Wednesday. The meeting date at Canterbury was therefore set for the 16th.

seid princes were so enpoverysshed that they hadde not sufficient of lyvelode ne of goodis, wherby they myght kepe and mayntene theire honorable estate and ordinarie charges withynne this realme.

Also the seid seducious persones, not willing to leve the possessions that they hadde, caused the seid princes to lay suche imposicions and charges as welle by way of untrue appecementes to whom they owed evill wille unto, as by dymes, taxis and prestis noblis and other inordinat charges uppon theire subjettes and commons, to the grete grugge and enpoveryssyng of them, wheche caused alle the people of this lond to grugge.

And also the seid seducious persones by theyre mayntenaunces, where they have rule, wold not suffre the lawes to be executed, but where they owe favour moved the seid princes to the same; by the wheche there were no lawes atte that tyme deuly ministred, ne putt in execucion, wheche caused gret murdres, roberyes, rapes, oppressions, and extorcions, as well by themself, as by theyre gret mayntenaunces of them to be doon, to the gret grugge of all this lande.

Hit is so that where the kyng oure sovereigne lorde hathe hadde as gret lyvelode and possessions as evyr had kyng of Engelond; that is to say, the lyvelode of the Crowne, Principalite of Wales, Duche of Lancastre, Duche of Cornwelle, Duche of York, the Erldome of Chestre, the Erldome of Marche, the Lordeschippe of Irlond, and other, with grete forfaytis, besyde Tunage and Poundage of alle this londe, grauntyd only to the kepynge of the see. The lorde Revers, the Duchesse of Bedford his wyf, and thayre sonnes, Ser William Harbert, Earle of Pembroke, and Humfrey Stafford, Erle of Devonshire, the Lord of Audely, and Ser John Fogge, and other of thayre myschevous assent and oppinion, whiche have advised and causid oure seid sovereigne lord to geve of the seyd lyvelode and possessions to them above theire disertis and degrees. So that he may nat lyf honorably and mayntene his estate and charges ordinarie withinne this lond.

And also the seid seducious persones next before expressid, not willyng to leve suche large possessions and goodis as they have of oure seid sovereigne lordis gyfte, have, by subtile and discevable ymaginacions, movid and causid oure sovereyne lord to chaunge his most ryche coyne, and mynysshed his most royalle household, to the gret appeycyng of his estate, and the comonwele of this londe.

Also seid seducious persones, continuyng in theire most deseyvable and covetous disposiscion, have causid oure seid soverayne lord to aske and charge us his trewe comons and subgettis wyth suche gret imposicions and inordinat charges, as by meanes of borowyng withoute payment, takyng goodes of executours of rich men, taxis, dymes, and preestis noblis; takyng gret goodis for his household without payment, impechementes of treasounes to whom they owe any eville will; So that ther can be no man of worshippe or richesse, other spirituelle or temporelle, knyghtis, squiers, marchauntes, or any other honest persone, in surete of his lyf, lyvelode, or goodis, where the seid seducious persones, or any of them, owe any malice or eville wille, to the grete drede and importabylle charges, and the utter empoverysshyng of us his treue Commons and subjettes. And to the gret enrychyng of themself, the premisses amountynge to ccMl. markes [this yere] and more.

Also the seid seducious persones have caused our seid sovereygne lord to spende the goodis of oure holy fadir [the pope], the wheche were yevyn liym for defence of Cristen feyth of many goodely disposyd people of this lond, without repayment of oure seid holy fadir, for the wheche cause this lond stondith in juberdie of Enterdytynge.

Also the seid seducious persones, be thayre mayntenaunces in the cuntreyes where they dwelt or where they here rule, will not suffre the Kynges lawes to be executyd uppon whom they owyd favere unto, And also movid oure seid sovereyne lord to the same; by the wheche the lawes be not duly mynystered, ne put in execucion; by the wheche gret murdre, robbres, rapes, oppressions, and extorcions, as well be them, as by thayre gret mayntenaunces of theire servauntes, to us daly done and remayne unpunysshed, to the gret hurt and grugge of alle this londe.

Also the seid seducious persones hath causid oure seid soverayne lord to estrainge the true lordis of his blood from his secrete Councelle, to th'entent that they myghte atteyne and brenge abought theyre fals and dysceyvable purpos in premisses aforseid, to the gret enrychynge of themselves, And to the gret hurt and poverte of oure seid sovereyne lorde, and to alle us his trewe subjettis and commons of this londe.

[End of Extract]

The Coventry Leet Book or Mayor's Register

The Early English Text Society, 1907 ed by Mary Dormer Harris

Extract from pages 340 - 346

TREASONS AND REBELLIONS.

By the kyng.

Trusty & welebylovyd, we grete yow well; & where we comwyttyd John Bawdewyn off Dortmowthe, cordwainere, vnto yowre warde for that he deliueryd in this oure Royaume a lettre wherinne was comprisyd treason, we vndyrstond now that he was not knowyng to the conteneu of the sayd lettre, but of innocence & simplenesse deliueryd it; wherfore & for that vs thinkyth that he hathe hade longe punusshement for hys said foly, we woll that incontynent apon the sight here-of, ye deliuer hym quite owt of prison, onlasse tha ye have other cause of keping them.

This yeuen undur oure signet at oure castell of Wyndesore the xvij day of May.

A pryvy seall sende to the meyr the iiij day of Juyll anno ix.

By the king.

Trusty & wilbylovyd, we grete you wel; & for-asmuche as it ys come to our knowlache that dyyers malicious & ille disposyd persones, contrari vnto God & theirs dueties, have cast & sowe in many & dyuers places of this our reaume, and yit continue dayly, vnfittyng and sedicious tales and langage amongus oure lege people to thentent to store and incens theym to rumour & commocion, not only to the grete offense off God & of their legens but also contrary to our lawes and pece & the comyn wele and pollicie of thys owr lande ; the whych, as we have cause, take to grete displeasir : We wol & in the straytyst wyse charge yow that ye, by alle wayes and meanes to yow possible, put you in ful deuoire and diligence that yffe any suche sedicious folke come or may be fonde within yowr jurisdiccion, ye put theym vndyr a-rest and sure warde so to remaigne vn-to the tyme we be sertefyed theroff by yowe, yevyng yow in comantlement what shall be do forthermore for their punysshement in that parte; not faylyng as ye love vs, and tendre the comune welfare off all this our reamne & subgettis of the same.

Yeven vnder our priue seal at our castell of Foderinghey the fyist day of Juyll.

By the kyng,

A letter yndur the kyngus signet sende to the meyre the X day of Juyll anno ix

Trusty & wilbyloved, we grete well; & for-as- muche as be fully determynyd to goo at this time in propre personne into the north parties of this our reame for the suppressing of suche ryottes as ben dayly committid there, as well in assemblyng of our people as in makyng proclamacions contrary to ther legens, & our pece; we therefore desire & pray yow that in all hast possibyl after the sight of thies out letters ye sende onto vs C archers well and defensible arayd to assist vs to the entent a-fore-sayde ; not faylyng herof as oure esp[ec]ial trust is in yow, & as ye tendre the wele of vs & of owre sayd reame.

Yeven vndyr out signet at our town of Stanford the v day of Juyll.

A lettre sende to the meyre fro my lord of Warwic the xij day of Juyll.

Ryhgt trusty and wil-belovyd frende [see duplicate for continuation[1]].

A lettre sende by therle of Warwyk to his seryondis & wolwyllers[2] within the cyte of Covyntre the xij day of Juyn[3] anno regis ix.

Ryhgt trusty and welfe-bylouyd, I grete you wele. Forasmiche as hyt hath pleasyd the kinges gode grace to sende at this tyme for hys lordis & other his subgettis to atende a-pon hys hyghnes northward, & that bothe the rihgt hye & mihgty prince, my lord the duke of Clarens, & I ben fully purposid, after the solempnizacion of the maryage by Goddes grace in short tyme to be hadde bitwene my sayd lord and my dohgter, to awayte on the same & to drawe vnto oure sayd soueren lord highues, I therfore desire & pray yow that ye woll in the meenetyme yeve knowlache to all suche felisshypp as ye mowe make (toward them[4]) to arredy theym in the best wyse they can, & that bothe ye & they defensibly arrayd be redy apon a day's warning to acompany my sayd lord & me towardes the sayd highnes, as my speciall trust ys in yow, yevyng credens to this berer in that he shall open vnto yow on my bihalue; and owre lord haue yow in hys keping.

Writon at London the xxviij[5] day of Juyn.

Therle of Warwyk & Salisbure, grete chamburlayn of England & capten of Calais.
R.Warwyk

---

[1] Two letters sent to Coventry by Warwick, one to the Mayor and one to his servants & followers. There are only minor differences. Text of latter letter given above.
[2] Followers.
[3] Should be July, as Mayor's letter.
[4] Words in brackets in Mayor's version.
[5] xxvij in Mayor's version.

By the kyng.

A letter sende the xiij day of Juyll.

Trusty & wele-bylovyd, we grete yow well; and woll and charge yow that Inmediatly after the sihgt of this oure letters ye sende vnto us suche men in defensibly array as we late wrete vnto yow fore, with moe if ye godly may, without fayling, alle expenses leyde a-parte, apon the faith & ligeance ye owe vnto vs ; & that in no wyse ye make any rising or assemblees with any persone what-so-euer he bee, nor suffre any of oure subgettes within our Cite of Coventre to doo apon the sayd payne, withowt that we vndir our priue seal or signet or signe manuell commande yow to doo.

Yeven vndyr oure signet at Newerk the X day of Juyll.

Those persons folowyng grauntyd 1 marke for 1 sowders for xx days to go to the kyng to Yorke a-gayns Robyn of Ryddesdale anno ix.

Will Sandurs, maior, Hen. Boteler, recordator, Ric. Wode, Ric. Braytofft, Edm. Brogreve, Rob. Brodmedewe, Joh. Wyldgrys, Tho. Brodmedewe, Will. Pere, Joh. Ruyton, Joh. Pynchbek, Joh. Gage, Will. Dawe, Ric. Colyns, Job. Stevyns, Joh. Bette, Ric Awstyn, Joh. Garton, Ric. Aide, Will. Horsley, Will. Stafford, Joh. Bayly, Rob. Atturton, Tho. Dowve, Symkyn Byrches, Tho. Broke, Tho. Forde, Joh. Hoton, Joh. Hadley de Flete-stret. Job. Semon, Joh. Grove, Tho. Strawnge, Will. Kokkes, Will. Knyhgt, Rog. Glouer, Joh. Fysher, Will Jawderell, Ric. Rede, baker, Tho. Wolffe, Ric. Bower, Tho. Napton, Rob. Bumell, Tho. Tate, Joh. Strange, G[r]eg. Heyne, Har. Barfote, Joh. Shemyn, Rafe Walker, Joh. Hastyng, Will. Bedon, Ric. Bedon, Hen. Banbere, Tho. Ruyton, Will. Pynchebek, Joh. Dorlyng, (no first name) Dorlyng, weuer, Joh. Arowe, Tho. Potell, Tho. Colyns, Joh. Philypp, Tho. Gryme, Joh. Bordale, Edm. Hadley, (no first name) Coke, Sadler, Philyp Robartes, Will. Rowley, Petrvs Clerkeson, Joh. Bladsmybtb, Tho. Campyon, Ric. Edward, Tho. Roby, Joh. Hazard, Will. Branche, Lawr. Sandurs, Ric. Cokkes, baker, Lawr. Walgrave, Tho. Hyton, (no first name) Huet, weucr, (no first name) Huet, corveser, Ric. Wylson, (no first name) Godknave, cowper, (no first name) Watford, girdeler.[6]

After thys grante they cowthe gete noe sowdere vndyr X d. a day, & so they were payd.

Collectores[7] *de Gosford warde* : Rog. Glouer, Joh. Hastyng, Law. Sandurs. [£3. 17s. 4d.]

Jurden-Well : Joh. Walton, Kic Brake, Hen. Gefferey. [£2. 13s. 4d.]

---
[6] 82 names in total.
[7] Amounts of money collected by ward to pay for the soldiers.

Muche-parke-strete : Joh. Wylde, Ric. Fletcher, Rob. Crosse, Joh. Smyth. [£3. 6s. 8d.]
Irle-strete : Ric. Alen, Joh. Swan, Rob. Jokys. [£4. 0s. 4d.]
Baly-lone: Ric. Wylson, Joh. Castell, Joh. Gryme. [£2. 11s. 2d.]
Brod-yate: Hen. Mason, Tho. Ruyton, Hug. Glouer. [£1. 13s. 5d.]
Smythford: Ric. Drowthe, Joh. Oldbere, Joh. Toty. [£2. 13s. 4d.]
Spon strete : Joh. Emettes Will. Godeladde, Ric Tornour. [£3. 15s. 10d.]
Croschepyng : Tho. Gardnere, Nye. Rondull, Will. Bolewyke. [£5. 1s. 2d.]
Bysshopp-strete warde : Ric. Cokkes, baker, Joh. Yale, Tho. Hyton. [£3, 15s. 4d.]
Summa xxxiij li. vij s. xj d. [£33 7s 11d]

Also Wyllyaw Sandnrs, meyre beynge at that tyme, yaffe of hys owne money to this jorney v li [£5]. in relesynge of pore men that shuld have bore here part to this costys Ward.

EDGCOTE FIELD AND AFTER.

Those be the namys of captens ordenyd in euery warde for the savegard of this cete:

Gosford warde : Joh. Wylgrys, Rob. Blewbere, Joh. Fulbroke, WilL Knyght, Will Cokkes, Joh. Stafford.

Jurden Wel-ward : Joh. Pynchebek, Ric. Alde, Will Stafford, Tho. Broke, Huwe Pollard, Joh. Fysher.

Muche-parke ward : Hen. Butler, Rob. Atturton, Rob. Onley, Joh. Wylde, Joh. Bordale, Rob. Tasker, Joh. Smyth, bacster.

Irle-stret ward: Ric. Wode, Rob. Brodmedew, Tho. Brodmedew, Joh. Gage, Will. Dawe, Tho. Ingram.

Brode-yate warde : Edm. Brogreve, Joh. Ruyton, Tho. Hawnell, Tho. Napton, Raffe Freman, Tho. Ruyton.

Smyt[h]ford warde : Ric. Braytofft, Ralf Caldbek, Job. Thruiwpton, Kic. Drowthe, Job. Toty, corveser, Ric. Bower.

Spon strete warde : Tho. Dowve, Joh. Shyrwode, Joh. Hadley, Job. Smythe, Will. Pynchebek, Ric. Everdon.

Croschepyng: Will. Peer, Joh. Bette, Will. Horsley, Will Marshall, Rob. Burnell, Nye. Rondell.

Bysshop-strete warde : Joh. Hadley, Will. Baxster, Joh. Mores, Law. Walgrave, Joh. Yale, Rog. Browne.

Bayly-lane : Joh. Bayly, Tho. Hobbes, Tho. Gryme, Joh. Castell, Joh. Gryme, Gef. Ardurn.

Delyuered to Rob. Onley on Mawdelyn day[8] a. r. ix a serpentyne with the chambur for the New-yate, & a hande gunne with a pyke in the ynde and a fowler.

Item, delyueryd to Joh. Hadley the same day for the Byssop-yate j staffe gunne & a [blank].

Item, delyuered to Will. Saundurs, meyre, ij staffe gunnes & a grett gunne wih, iij cbamburs, iij jackes, & xxiiij arowys; redepti iiij jackes and xxiiij arowys.

Item, delyueryd to Joh. Wylgrys j gunne with iij chamburs lyggyng at the towr to the Fryres garden.

Item, delyueryd to the Byssbopp-yate by Joh. Hoton a fowler.

Item, to Ric. Wode iij jacket & ij dosen arowes.

Item, delyueryd to Joh. Semon j newe jacke & a olde.

By the kynge.

Trusty & wel-belouyd, we grete yow wele, and thanke yow ryhgt hertly of the feythfull deuoir that ye haue put yow in at this tyme in sending to vs of suche felashipp out of our Cite of Couentre, to vs rihgt a-greable as ye haue don, wherby ye haue shewyd yow of tendre zele and effeccion to the wele & seurty of oure person to owre grete pleasir, which with (illeg) olde aproued tr[e]wthe vnto vs heretofor we haue and euer will haue in oure tendre and herty remembrans. And for the same haue causyd vs to haue yow, as soo we wil, in the more trust and fauorable recommendacion at al tymes hereafter in any thing that we may doo for the wele of you & of oure said Citie in suche wise as ye shall thenke youre sayd acquitail and service rihgt wel byset with Goddes grace.

Yeuen vndre oure signet at oure towne of Notynham the xxix day of Juyll.

(The following section is a translation of a Memorandum written in Latin, provided in the original publication)

Memorandum: Lord Herbert was taken in a battle by Banbury with Robin of Redesdale and his fellows on S. James' Eve 1469, and was taken to Northampton, and there beheaded, and Lord Richard Herbert likewise with others.

Item On Aug. 12 in the same year Lord Rivers then Treasurer of England was beheaded at Gosford Green, and Lord John Woodville, his son, likewise; they had been taken at Chepstow.

Item Lord Southwick was taken at Bridgewater and there beheaded.

Item Lord Humfrey Neville, knight, was beheaded in the north country in the same year, and his brother Charles and the bailiff of Durham at the same time.

[End of Extract]

---

[8] Magdelene Day is 22nd July.

The Paston Letters 1422-1509 Volume 5

Chatto and Windus, 1904 ed by James Gairdner

Extract from pages 35 - 36, Letter 719

EDWARD IV. TO THE DUKE OF CLARENCE, &c. 1

These iij. letteres undirwreten, the Kyng of his own hand wrote unto my Lords Clarence, Warrewyke, and Archbishop of York. The credence wherof in substaunce was, that every of them shulde in suech pesibil wise, as thei have be accustumed to ryde, come unto his Highness.

R. E.

To our Brother of Clarence.

BRODIR, we pray you to yeve feight [faith] and credence to our welbeloved Sir Thomas Montgomery and Morice Berkly, in that on our behalf thei shal declare to you. And we truste ye wole dispose you accordyng to our pleser and comaundement. And ye shal be to us right welcome.

At Notyngham the ix. day of Jull.

To our Cosyn Th'erl of Warr'.

COSYN, we grete you well, and pray you to yeve feight and credence to Sir Thomas Mongomery and Morice Berkley, &c. And we ne trust that ye shulde be of any suech disposicion towards us, as the rumour here renneth, consederyng the trust and affeccion we bere in yow. At Notyngham the ix. day of Jull. And, cosyn, ne thynk but ye shalbe to us welcome.

To our Cosyn Th' archbyshop of Yorke.

COSYN, we pray you that ye wul, accordyng to the promyse ye made us, to come to us as sone as ye goodely may. And that [ye] yeve credence to Sir Thomas Mongomery and Morice Berkly, in that un our behalve thei shal sey to you; and ye shalbe to us welcome. At Notyngham the ix. day of Jul.

[End of Extract]

Marwnad Wiliam Herbert o Raglan, iarll cyntaf Penfro

Elegy for William Herbert of Raglan, first earl of Pembroke

By Guto'r Glyn.

Edited by Barry J Lewis. Taken from www.gutorglyn.net.

1 Dawns o Bowls! Doe'n ysbeiliwyd,
2 Dyn yr holl dynion i'r rhwyd.
3 Dawns gwŷr Dinas y Garrai,
4 Dawns yr ieirll: daw'n nes i rai!

5 Duw Llun y bu waed a lladd,
6 Dydd amliw, diwedd ymladd.
7 Duw a ddug y dydd dduw Iau
8 Iarll Dwywent a'r holl Deau.

9 Marchog a las dduw Merchyr,
10 Mwy ei ladd no mil o wŷr:
11 Syr Rhisiart, ni syr Iesu
12 Wrthaw er lladd North a'r llu.
13 Duwmawrth gwae ni am Domas:
14 Duw Llun gyda'i frawd y'i llas.
15 Dwyn yr iarll a'i bedwarllu,
16 Dydd Farn ar anrhydedd fu.
17 Arglwydd difwynswydd Defnsir
18 A ffoes – ni chafas oes hir!
19 Bradwyr a droes brwydr a drwg
20 Banbri i'r iarll o Benbrwg.

21 Cad drycin am y drin draw

22 Carliaid a wnaeth y curlaw.
23 Ymladd tost am laddiad hwn
24 A wna'r hynt yn Norhantwn.

---

1 The Dance of Death! Yesterday[1] we were despoiled,
2 the snatching up of all the men into the net.
3 The dance of the men of Doncaster,
4 the dance of the earls: to some it will come closer yet!

5 On Monday there was blood and slaughter,
6 a day of disgrace, the end of all fighting.
7 On Thursday God took away
8 the earl of both regions of Gwent and all south Wales.

9 On Wednesday a knight[2] was killed,
10 killing him was a greater thing than a thousand of any other men:
11 Sir Richard, Jesus won't be angry with him
12 for killing the Northerners and the host.
13 On Tuesday woe for us because of Thomas[3],
14 on Monday he was killed beside his brother.
15 The taking of the earl and his four hosts,
16 it was the Day of Judgement upon honour.
17 The lord of Devon, his service was worthless,
18 fled – he didn't live long!
19 It was traitors who brought down
20 the battle and the evil of Banbury upon the earl of Pembroke.

21 We have endured savage weather on account of the fighting over there,
22 it was churls who caused the lashing rain.
23 The expedition to Northampton will bring about
24 fierce fighting on account of the killing of this man.

---

[1] According to the translator it is traditional in elegies to refer to the death as occurring "yesterday".
[2] Sir Richard Herbert.
[3] Thomas Vaughan who died in the battle. See later poem for his elegy.

25 Awn oll i ddial ein iaith	25 Let us all go to avenge our nation
26 Ar ddannedd y Nordd unwaith	26 in the teeth of the Northerners at once,
27 A dyludwn hyd Lydaw	27 and let us pursue as far as Brittany
28 Dan draed y cyffredin draw.	28 the commoners there beneath our feet.
29 Ef â'r gwŷr a fu ar gam	29 All the men who were in the wrong,
30 Oll i ddiawl, yn lladd Wiliam.	30 killing William, will go to the devil.
31 O rhoed, lle bu anrhydedd,	31 If weapon or sword was placed, where once was honour,
32 Ar fwnwgl iarll arf neu gledd,	32 upon an earl's neck,
33 Och Fair, cnodach fu arwain	33 alas, Mary, it was more usual once
34 Aerwy mawr o aur a main.	34 for it to bear a great collar of gold and gemstones.
35 Doe 'dd aeth dan y blaned ddu	35 Yesterday he departed under the black planet
36 Drwy'r fâl draw i ryfelu.	36 on his way through the valley there to make war.
37 Och finnau – uwch yw f'anun –	37 Alas for me – my sleeplessness is all the greater
38 Nad arhôi 'n ei dir ei hun.	38 - that he did not remain in his own land.
39 Ymddiried i'r dynged wan	39 It was faith in feeble fate
40 A'i twyllodd o Went allan.	40 which lured him out of Gwent.
41 Tair merched, tair tynged ton	41 Three women, three misshapen fates
42 Y sy'n dwyn oes ein dynion:	42 take away the life of our men:
43 Un a gynnail cogeilyn,	43 one holds a distaff,
44 Arall a nydd dydd pob dyn,	44 a second weaves the number of every man's days,
45 Trydedd yn torri edau	45 a third cuts a thread
46 Er lladd iarll a'r llu dduw Iau.	46 to kill an earl and the host on Thursday.
47 Mynnwn fy mod ymannos	47 I wish I had been the other night
48 Yn torri pen Atropos.	48 cutting off the head of Atropos.
49 Nid rhan i'r tair a henwais	49 The three women whom I've named
50 Nyddu oes hir yn nydd Sais.	50 don't get to weave a long life while there's an Englishman around.
51 Os gwir i blant Alis gau,	51 If it's true that Alice's treacherous children[4],
52 Draeturiaid, dorri tyrau,	52 the traitors, have felled men who were towers,
53 Ni ddôi'r iangwyr, ni ddringynt	53 the churls wouldn't have dared, they wouldn't have climbed
54 I dai'r gŵr na'i dyrau gynt.	54 into his house before now, nor his towers.
55 Gwinllan fu Raglan i'r iaith,	55 Raglan was a vineyard for the nation,
56 Gwae ni wŷl ei gwin eilwaith!	56 woe to him who shall never see its wine again!
57 Gwae a weles ar Galan	57 Woe to him who saw on New Year's Day
58 Gynnal gwledd ar ganol glan!	58 a feast being held at the heart of the waterside!
59 Gwae a geisio rhodio rhawg	59 Woe to him who may try from now on
60 Gwent dlawd oedd gynt oludawg!	60 to ply his way through Gwent which was once so wealthy![5]

---

[4] i.e. The English.
[5] The poet is lamenting the loss of a generous patron and future commissions.

61 Ei farw oedd well i fardd iach	61 It would be better for a poet sound in body but without his sanity,
62 Heb ei bwyll, no byw bellach.	62 to die rather than to live longer.
63 Merddin Wyllt am ei urddas,	63 Myrddin the Wild, son of Morfryn[6],
64 Amhorfryn, aeth i'r glyn glas.	64 for his lost honour withdrew to the green valley.
65 Af yn wyllt o fewn elltydd	65 I too will go wild in woodlands
66 I eiste rhwng clustiau'r hydd.	66 to sit between the ears of a stag.
67 Ef a'm llas, mi a'm nasiwn,	67 I was killed, I and my nation too,
68 Yr awr y llas yr iarll hwn,	68 the moment that this earl was killed,
69 Cymro oedd yn ffrwyno Ffrainc,	69 a Welshman who used to bridle France
70 Camreol Cymry ieuainc.	70 and the misrule of young Welshmen.
71 Ofn i bawb tra fu 'n y byd,	71 He inspired fear in all while he was in the world,
72 Yn iach ofn oni chyfyd!	72 farewell to fear now unless he comes back to life!
73 Ymgyrchu i Gymru a gân',	73 They will be able to march on Wales now,
74 Ymsaethu 'm Mhowys weithian.	74 to make arrow-play in Powys.
75 Doed aliwns, nis didolir,	75 Let aliens come, they won't be driven away,
76 O dôn', pwy a'u lludd i dir?	76 if they do come, who will stop them landing?
77 Llusgent wŷr, llosgent eu tai,	77 Let them drag men away, let them burn their houses,
78 Lladdwyd y gŵr a'u lluddiai.	78 the man who might stop them has been killed.
79 Traws eto rhag trais atyn'	79 A strong man against oppression, yet, to face them,
80 Tra ater Syr Rhosier ynn.	80 so long as Sir Roger[7] is left to us.
81 Trimaib iarll, os trwm y byd,	81 Three earl's sons, if the world is grievous,
82 Tri a ostwng ein tristyd.	82 three will assuage our grief.
83 Un o'i hil yn Neheuwlad	83 One of his offspring in the South
84 A gyrredd dwyn gradd ei dad.	84 will win the same rank as his father.
85 Iarll oedd, Cymru oll eiddo,	85 He was an earl, all Wales was his,
86 Iarll o'i fab arall a fo!	86 let another earl yet come from his son!

---

[6] Refers to another poet who went mad when his patron was killed.
[7] Pembroke's half brother, and brother of Thomas Vaughan. He was killed in 1471.

Marwnad Tomas ap Syr Rhosier Fychan

Elegy for Thomas son of Sir Roger Vaughan

By Lewys Glyn Cothi.

The Welsh edited text is taken from Dafydd Johnston (ed.), Gwaith Lewys Glyn Cothi (University of Wales Press, Cardiff, 1995), poem 124. This translation was prepared especially for this publication by Professor Ann Parry Owen of the University of Wales Centre for Advanced Welsh and Celtic Studies. Northamptonshire Battlefields Society is extremely grateful for her efforts and support in bringing this important work to a wider audience.

1 Y maes grymusa' o Gred,	1 The most mighty battlefield of Christendom,
2 ac o wall ef a golled;	2 and it was lost through a failing[1];
3 ym Manbri y bu'r dial	3 the vengeance upon fair Wales
4 ar Gymru deg a'r mawr dâl;	4 was exacted at Banbury at great cost;
5 yno clywid yn unawr	5 there, all at once, was heard
6 griaw maes rhwng gweywyr mawr;	6 the crying of battle amongst large spears;
7 rhai Herbart, rhai'n Edwart ni,	7 some [crying for] Herbert, others for our Edward,
8 Iarll Warwig, eraill Harri.	8 the Earl of Warwick, and others for Harry.
9 Dan faner arglwydd Herast	9 The breach, the injury and the clash (lit. 'touch')
10 y bu'r tor a'r briw a'r tast;	10 happened under the banner of the lord of Hergest;
11 Tomas, rhwng y dwysias ddig,	11 Thomas son of Roger with the shattered spear
12 ap Rhosier â'r pâr ysig.	12 was located between the two wrathful armies.
13 Arthur pan fu'n ei guras,	13 Arthur when he was wearing his cuirass
14 ymlaen llu Camlan y llas,	14 was struck down leading a host at Camlann,
15 ac yntau'i hun, ac nid hawdd,	15 and he [Arthur], single handedly, and this wasn't easy,
16 â dwylaw a'i dialawdd.	16 took revenge for this with his own hands.
17 Tomas a las fal Iesu,	17 Thomas was killed like Jesus,
18 a phan las, a phen ei lu,	18 and when he was killed, along with the leader of his army,
19 Tomas yn ei guras gwyn	19 Thomas, in his white[2] cuirass,
20 a'i talodd hwnt i'w elyn.	20 exacted vengeance for this on his enemy.
21 Petai ddwrn tradwrn â'r tri	21 Had it been fist to fist with the three
22 mwya' unbraint ym Manbri,	22 most dignified ones at Banbury,

---

[1] This may refer to the Earl of Devon's infamous actions.
[2] The word in Welsh means "White" but can be read as shining/brilliant for metals, with the context of "very good" or "excellent" as well.

23 ef a wnâi a wnelai naw	23 he [Thomas] would have accomplished the work of nine
24 wedy'r ellwng law drallaw.	24 once hands had been set on hands[3]
25 Ni chafas, lle llas y llall,	25 At the place where the other was killed, he did not receive
26 gwir gwyr â gwr ac arall,	26 a single combat, man to man,
27 a phei cawsoedd, lle'dd oedd ddau,	27 and if he had received a single combat,
28 gwir gwyr, ef a gâi'r gorau.	28 where there were two of them, he would have been victorious.
29 Ban fu fatel ein gelyn	29 When our enemy's army
30 ym Manbri oer ym mhen bryn,	30 was on a hilltop at wretched Banbury,
31 deuwr aeth, ni chad yr un,	31 two men went, neither returned,
32 iarll Gwent, arall o Gintun.	32 the earl of Gwent, and the other from Kington[4].
33 Yr oedd ar ŵyr Foriddig	33 The descendent of Moriddig
34 gampau oedd dda heb gamp ddig.	34 was endowed with abilities having achieved no bitter accomplishment.
35 Ni fynnodd yn ei faenawr	35 In his manor he never insisted
36 drwy waith efô un dreth fawr.	36 intentionally upon high taxation,
37 ond gwared ar gyffredin	37 but rather on helping the common people
38 a rhannu oll i'r rhain win.	38 and on sharing his wine with all of them.
39 Rhyfeddod llyfr gwybodol	39 It would be the miracle of a learned book
40 fyw y neb a fai'n ei ôl.	40 that anyone were to survive after losing him.
41 Elen Gethin fu'n wylaw	41 Elen Gethin[5] wept
42 ddefni gwlith yn ddafnau glaw,	42 drops of dew as drops of rain,
43 ac o'r wylaw gwrolaeth	43 and after the weeping following his death
44 fry yn ôl ei farw a wnaeth.	44 she performed a valiant feat.
45 Hi a wnaeth yn hyn o wyl	45 She organised this festival for him[6]
46 yn Herast i hwn arwyl.	46 in Hergest as his funeral feast.
47 Wedy hwn y dihunant,	47 Following him will awake
48 dri fal Siors a Derfel Sant.	48 the three who are like George or St Derfel.
49 Mae'r tri ar fedr ei ddial,	49 The three are intent on avenging him,
50 mae un Duw'n rhoi i minnau dâl:	50 and the One God provides me with recompense:
51 Maestr Watcyn, fap impyn pêr,	51 Master Watkin, the son who is a handsome offshoot,
52 Maestr Rhisiart a Maestr Rhosier.	52 Master Richard and Master Roger.
53 Amcen trimeib Custennin	53 [Three men] with the objective of Constantine's three sons

---

[3] i.e. once battle had commenced.
[4] This means Thomas Vaughan.
[5] Thomas Vaughan's wife, and an interesting character in her own right.
[6] This suggests that the poem was performed in his funeral feast, at Hergest.

54 a fu wŷr traw i fwrw trin.
55 Wynt-hwy ddielyn' eu tad
56 ar Loegr cyn hun ar lygad,
57 a'r rhain cyn nemor o haf
58 a ry maes o'r grymusaf,
59 a'r ddeuddydd newydd yn un
60 a roddo Mab Mair uddun'.
61 Mewn y lle a'r man y llas
62 Duw a ymwan am Domas.
63 Delw Fair a'i diail efô,
64 Duw eilwaith a'i dialo.

54 who were staunch soldiers overthrowing battle.
55 They will wreak vengeance for their father
56 against England before sleep overtakes the eye,
57 and, hardly before summer has arrived, these
58 will wage the mightiest of battles,
59 and may the Son of Mary give to them
60 the two days as one.
61 At the place and the location where he was killed,
62 God will fight for Thomas.
63 The image of Mary will avenge him,
64 and may God also avenge him.

Marwnad Wiliam Herbert

Elegy for William Herbert

By Hywel Swrdwal.

The Welsh edited text is taken from Dylan Foster Evans (ed.), Gwaith Hywel Swrdwal a'i Deulu (Centre for Advanced Welsh and Celtic Studies, Aberystwyth, 2000), poem 7. This translation was again prepared by Professor Ann Parry Owen.

1 Ni bo i berchen bwa
2 Racw'n swydd Iorc unnos dda,
3 Ac ni bo yno annedd
4 Undyn byw ond yn y bedd.
5 O dof uwchben ei hennyth
6 Ni werthaf ŵr o'r North fyth.
7 Mawr yw'n angof a'n gofid,
8 Am iarll o Went y mae'r llid.
9 Nid oedd—pam y'i diweddent?—
10 Ŵr well ei gorff no iarll Gwent.

11 Nid oedd well yn Lloegr chwellaw
12 No'i frodyr, Iarll Penfro, draw:
13 Syr Rhisiart, Tomas ryswr,
14 Siôn wych a'i profes yn ŵr.
15 Dechrau breninbrennau'n bro,
16 Dodi'r wadd i'w dadwreiddio.

17 Bwriad a gwaith a brad gwŷr
18 Banbri ydoedd, ben-bradwyr.
19 Dwy gynneddf oll, dygnedd fu,
20 Ar Saeson a roes Iesu:
21 Lolardiaid, traeturiaid hen
22 Ŷnt erioed, ânt i'r wden!
23 Troasant eiriau Iesu,
24 Traeturiaid ŷnt i'r tarw du.
25 Ni rôi Sais yn yr oes hon

1 Let there not be a single good night
2 for the owner of a bow yonder in Yorkshire,
3 and let there not be there a home
4 for any man lest it be in a grave.
5 Should I come to his old hiding-place
6 I will never ransom a man from the North[1].
7 Great is our oblivion and our sorrow,
8 our anger being for the earl of Gwent.
9 There was no better man of physique
10 – why did they put an end to him? – than the earl of Gwent.

11 There were no six hands in England better
12 than the brothers of the earl of Pembroke.
13 Sir Richard, the champion Thomas,
14 excellent John who proved himself a man.
15 To begin with, the mole[2]
16 was sent to uproot the largest trees[3] of our land.

17 A conspiracy, an act, and the betrayal of men
18 at Banbury by chief-traitors.
19 Jesus endowed the English with
20 only two qualities, a cause of distress:
21 they have always been Lollards,
22 traitors of old, they will go to the noose!
23 They have perverted the words of Jesus,
24 they are traitors of the black bull.[4]
25 No Englishman in this age

---

[1] i.e. I will kill him outright.
[2] The Earl of Warwick. The mole was often the symbol for the enemy in prophetic poetry. It will later be used to described Richard III.
[3] i.e. Leaders.
[4] George, Duke of Clarence's symbol was the Black Bull as was Edward IV's. This could refer to those betraying Edward, or the traitors working with Clarence.

26 Drugaredd i du'r Goron.	26 would show mercy towards the Crown.
27 Trech anian ym mhob rhan rhôm	27 Amongst us, in all parts, nature is stronger
28 Nog addysg, ni a'i gwddom.	28 than nurture, we know this.
29 Tebyg iawn at beganiaid	29 They are very similar to pagans,
30 Ydynt wy, Waden eu taid.	30 Woden[5] was their ancestor.
31 Tebyg iawn eto heb gam	31 On the other hand, William,
32 I Dduw eilwaith oedd Wiliam.	32 free of any injustice, was very similar to God.
33 Edward wyn, dyred unwaith	33 Blessed Edward, come sometime
34 I Gymru i enynnu'n iaith.	34 to Wales to ignite our nation.
35 Myn bawb, nid ymwan eb wŷr,	35 Ensure that everyone – there is no jousting without men –
36 Ar dy ôl, â'r dialwyr.	36 follows you along with the avengers.
37 Daly dy ffordd, dilid â ffust	37 Continue on your way, and with flails pursue
38 Hwrswns o Hors a Heinsiust.	38 the bastard sons of Horsa and Hengist.
39 Na ad wŷr yn y dwyrain,	39 In the east, beyond Banbury,
40 Banbri hwnt, ben byw o'r rhain.	40 do not leave a single one of them alive.
41 Digiwch fry'r Cymry rhag cam,	41 May you incite anger in the Welsh because of the injustice,
42 Dielwch, er Duw, Wiliam.	42 and, for God's sake, seek vengeance for William.
43 Llosgwch, na chiliwch i'ch ôl,	43 May you burn, do not retreat,
44 Swydd Loncastr a swydd Lincol.	44 the counties of Lancaster and Lincoln.
45 Byrhëwch, ffustiwch yn ffest,	45 May you shorten, and pummel hard,
46 Gyrff hirion gwŷr y Fforest.	46 the long bodies of the men of the Forest.[6]
47 Un Duw a wna, a Dewi,	47 In my opinion, the One God, and St David,
48 Am wŷr y North fy marn i,	48 will do the same with the men of the North;
49 Anffod a chernod a chas	49 may there be misfortune, a clash and enmity
50 I Gaerloyw, ac oer leas!	50 upon Gloucester, and cruel slaughter!
51 I chwerthin am y drin draw;	51 Laughter followed the battle yonder;
52 Trin eilwaith a'u tro'n wylaw.	52 another battle will turn them to sobbing.
53 Ar Iau 'dd aeth a urddai wŷr	53 It was on Thursday that the one whom men honoured[7] departed,
54 A'r marchog ar y Merchyr,	54 and the knight[8] went on the Wednesday,
55 A'i frodyr a'i wŷr eraill,	55 and he along with his brothers and other men,
56 Llu dduw Llun, yn lladd y llaill.	56 a host on the Monday, had been slaying the other [host].

---

[5] The early English kings, and the later Lancastrian kings especially, traced their ancestry to the pagan Woden. Edward the IV, on the other hand, descended from the Mortimers, Gwladus Ddu and Llywelyn the Great, and the Christian Cadwaladr the Blessed.
[6] This means the Forest of Dean.
[7] William Herbert.
[8] Sir Richard Herbert.

57 Nef i'r Cymry gwedy'r gis	57 Heaven for the Welsh following the clash
58 A diliw i waed Alis.	58 and ruin upon the blood of Alice[9].
59 Och na chefais, trais fu'r tro,	59 Woe that I did not receive the miracles of St Beuno[10]
60 Wrth ddau ben wrthiau Beuno	60 for the two heads, it was an act of violence,
61 Yn y modd, ni cheisiwn mwy,	61 in this way – I would not ask for more –
62 Y gwnâi fry â Gwenfrewy.	62 he would do as he did for St Winifrede.
63 Nid amlach main hyd Sain Siâm	63 No more numerous are the stones on the path to Santiago[11]
64 No'i foliant, nef i Wiliam.	64 than his praise - heaven for William.
65 Na fid Gymro drosto draw,	65 If he was good, let there not be a Welshman
66 O bu dda, heb weddïaw.	66 who does not pray for him.
67 O bu drwm, y byd a red,	67 If he was severe, as the world goes,
68 Maddeuent am ei ddäed.	68 may they forgive him on account of his goodness.
69 Ba ŵr a wŷl byw o'i ran	69 What living man will ever see his like
70 Byth ei gyffelyb weithian?	70 from now on?
71 Iawn o orchwyl ynn erchi	71 It is a fitting undertaking for us to demand
72 Roi gwledd nef i'n harglwydd ni,	72 that the heavenly feast will be given to our lord,
73 A'r rhif a fu farw hefyd	73 and that the number that died with him
74 I'r nef gydag ef i gyd.	74 all accompany him to heaven.

---

[9] i.e. the English. Alice was the daughter of Hengist, therefore *gwaed Alis* 'the blood of Alice' refers to the English
[10] Lines 59-62 refer to the miracle performed by St Beuno, who reattached St Winifrede's head to her body after she had been decapitated. This confirms that William and Richard Herbert were beheaded.
[11] Santiago de Compostelle in Spain, a major site of Pilgrimage.

Recueil des croniques et anchiennes istories de la Grant Bretaigne - Jean de Wavrin

Volume 6, Book 5, Chapter 47.

Aprez ce que le seigneur de Riviere et son fils furent partis de la court du roy il en fut moult doulent car moult les amoit; si appela les seigneurs de Hastings et de Mountjoy, messier Thomas Abouret et messier Thomas de Montgomery, ausquelz il demanda pour quell cause ceulz du North marchoient si avant en pays et sil estoit besoing quil se meist auz champs, lesquelz respondirent au roy que non, et que ce nestoit reins, ja sceussent ilz bein le contraire, parquoy le roy se asseura Qui ne scavoit pas le comte Pennebrocq este si prochain de luy, et on ne voulloit pas aussi quil le seust adfin quil ne se joindist avex lui, et pourtant sadvancerent secretement les annemis du roy le plus quilz peurent avant quil le sceust, et tant marcherent dun coste et dautre quilz arriverent prez duneville qui on nomme Theosbury, de la Londres environ quatrre vingtz milles, tant quil navoi entre les deux ostz que une petite riviere avec petite distance (guaires plus dune lieue), ou ilz geurent celle nuit. Et estoit conducteur pour ceulz du North le comte de Wilbie, adcompaignie dun villain nomme Robin Rissedale, capitaine de tout le commun; et du coste de ceulz de Galles y estoient messier Guillaume de Herbert, messier Henry son frere et messier Thomas leur emy frere, lequel morut a la besongne et les deux autres y furent prins. Ainsi doncques furent illec toute la nuit, et lendemain chascun de son coste sadvancha pour prevenir au passage de la riviere, mais oncques sitost ny parvindrent les Gallois quilz ny trouverent ceulz de North; si ny avoit amenemessire Guillaume de Herbert gueres de gens, ancores estoient ils de cheval, et avoit ceulz de pie laissies venir a leu raise derriere, car il ne cuidoit pas ceulz du North si prestz comme il fist, par lesquelz il fut constraint deffendre et garder le passage, ou il eut grosse escarmuche et moult de gens tuez; mais les Gallois tindrent le passage. Aprez que le Comte de Pennebrocq eut le pas concquis, ceulz du North se retrayrent, car ilz avoient beaucop perdu jusque a laprez disner que ilz atendoient le comte de Warewic, et aussi firent pareillement les Gallois pour atendre le residu de leurs gens. Mais quant ce vint aprez disner vindrent devers ceulz du North litigieusement deux chevaliers, lun estoit messier Guillamme Apparre et lautre messier Geffroy Guat lesquelz advertis de leur reboutement tantost les recoeillerent et ramenerent au passage, ou lescarmuche recommence moult grosse; pourquoy les Gallois y vindrent a puissance, mais ceulz du estoient beaucop plus grant nombre que les Gallles; et aussi quant le comte de Stamfort fut adcertene quele duc de Clarence venoit en layde de ceulz du North il hadandonna les Gallois et emmena avec luy de sept a huit mille hommes, pourquoy ceulz de Galles perdirent la journee, si en eut plusiers mors et prins, entre lesquelz y furent prisonniers comme dit a este cydessus les deux freres de Herbert. En ce tempore que ceulz du North et de Galles se combattoient, le duc de Clarence et le comte de Warewic estoient a Londres ou ilz faisoient passer ceulz de Kent cuidans venir assez a tempz a celle journee, mais non firent, car cestoit fait anchois quilz partissent de Londres, et ainsi que le comte de Warewic sappareilloit pour cuidier partir, Nouvelles lui vindrent que Gallois estoient ruez jus, dont il fut moult joieux; sy ne tarda gueres quant il se party et tyra vers Northanton ou il rencontra ceulz su North quy retournoient de celle besongne, pouquoy il fist alors retourner ceulz de Kent, lesquelz il remercya de leur bonne diligence et voullente.

Translation

Prepared by Livia Visser-Fuchs especially for the Northamptonshire Battlefields Society.

[Translators note: The French has been checked against the original, Bibliothèque nationale de France, ms fr. 85 The words in square brackets are the variants from another ms, BnF ms fr. 20358, f. 226r-v. This last ms is often slightly 'better' than the one used for the edited text.]

When Lord Rivers and his son[1] had left the King's court, he was very sad [for he loved them very much]; so he called the Lords Hastings and Mountjoy, Sir Thomas Burgh[Aburon] and Sir Thomas Montgomery and asked them why [and for what reason] the Northerners were thus marching into the country, and if it was necessary for him to take to the field; they replied to the King no, and that it was nothing, although they knew very well that the opposite was true. The King felt reassured [did not fear anything]: he did not know [at all] that the earl of Pembroke was so near him [as he was]; and they did not want to him to know so that he could not go and join him [them]. And therefore King's enemies advanced secretly as far as they could before he knew about it, and they marched from one direction and the other until they came to a town called Theosbury[2] about eighty miles from London, and all that was between the two hosts was a little river, only a small distance away, where they lay[?] that night[3].

Those from the North were lead by Lord Willoughby, accompanied by a villain called Robin of Rissedale, captain of all the common people; and on the side of the Welshmen was Sir William Herbert, Sir Henry, his brother, Sir Thomas their half brother, who was killed in the action and the other two were taken prisoner. Thus there they were all night, and the next day [in the morning] each side advanced to prevent the crossing of the river [to get to the crossing], but as soon as the Welsh arrived they found the Northerners already there; Sir William de Herbert had brought hardly any

---

[1] The beheading of Rivers and John Woodville ends the previous chapter, vol. 6, bk 5, ch. 46.
[2] Spelling almost the same in fr. 20358, but it is written like this the//osbery because it is on two lines.
[3] [and they camped so near each other that there was hardly more than a lieue between them, and there was between the two a little stream, and there they spent that night].

men and these were still on horseback, and he had allowed the foot soldiers to follow leisurely, for he did not think the Northmen would be as prepared as he found them[4]; and they forced him to defend the crossing and there was a great skirmish and many people were killed; but the Welsh held the crossing. After the earl of Pembroke had taken the crossing, the Northmen retreated, for they had lost many, until after dinner[5], as they waited for the earl of Warwick[6], and the Welsh did the same as they waited for the rest of their people.

But when 'after dinner' came two knights came to join the Northerners, ready to fight, one was Sir William Parr and the other Sir Geoffrey Gate, who, once they knew of the rebuff [of the Northerners][7], gathered them together and led them again to the crossing, where a very great skirmish started again; because of this the Welshmen came back in strength, but the Northerners had in much greater numbers than the Welsh; and when the 'count of Stamford[8]' heard [and was warned] that the duke of Clarence was coming to the aid of the Northerners he abandoned the Welsh and took with him seven or eight thousand men, because of which the Welsh lost the day; and there were several [many] killed and captured, among whom were taken prisoner, as said above, the two Herbert brothers.

At the time the Northerners and the Welshmen were fighting, the duke of Clarence and the earl of Warwick were in London, where they had the people of Kent go[9], thinking they would arrive in time for this day [of battle], but they did not[10] and it happened that when the earl of Warwick was making ready to leave, the news reached him that the Welshmen had been defeated, about which he was very glad; so he hardly delayed his departure and marched towards Northampton where he met the Northerners, who were returning from this business; therefore he allowed the men of Kent to go home and thanked them for their diligence and goodwill.

[End of Extract]

---

[4] [for he had left the footsoldiers behind, because he had not thought he would find the Northerners so near].
[5] 4 to 6 p.m.
[6] [because they waited for the earl of Warwick's people].
[7] [two knights, WP and GG, and when they arrive they realised and were informed that the Northerners had been beaten back].
[8] Humphrey Stafford.
[9] Instead of sending them by the shortest route to where the battle would take place?
[10] [for it was done before they left London.]

Extract from Dupont Edition Volume 3, Paris 1843.

Volume 6, Book 6 page 1 - 4

Quant doncqués le duc de Clarence et le Conte de Warewic se furent partis de Londres, eulz et tous leurs gens ilz ne st'arresterent tant qu'ilz vindrent Northanton: auquel lieu leur vint au devant le conte de Wilbie, qui leur presenta le seigneur de Herbert son frere; puis; quant ilz furent amenez devant le conte de Warewic, ilz encommencerent parler ensamble de gros languages, tant que le conte de Warewic commanda que on les emmenast morir. Et ainsi furent ces deus bons chevalliers livrez au peuple qui piteusement les lapiderent. Quant les seigneurs dessus nommez furent mors et ceulz de Galles ruez jus le roy en eut les nouvelles dont il fut moult desplaisant, si dist quil estoit trahy, et fist liabillier tous ses gens pour aller audevant de son frère le duc de Clarence et son cousin de Warewic lesquelz venoient audevant de luy et estoient desja entre Warewic et Conventry ou ilz furent advertis que le roy venoit a lencontre deulz. Et quant larchevesque dYorc sceut que le roy les aprochoit il dist au comte son frère quil latendist adfin que de riens ne se doubtast, mais feist on encqueste ou il se logeroit celle nuit. Le roy en chevaulchant venoit pensant a la mort des deux chevalliers devantdis, disant en soy mesmes quil se vengeroit de son frère de Clarence quy tel deshonneur luy avoit fait, et ainsi, moult pensif et desplaisant, chevaulcha tant quil vint a Conventry, ou il cuida logier, et de fait y avoit envoie ses fourriers pour prendre logis, mais ilz trouvèrent que les North avoient prins la place: si ne furent pas lesdis fourriers creuz dy prendre herberge, anchois furent bouttez hors de la ville, et pou sen failly quon ne les tua; pourquoy hastivement sen retournèrent devers le roy auquel ilz recorderent ce quilz avoient trouve, dont il fut moult mal meu, et eut conseil de non aller plus avant jusques ad ce que plus a plain feust imforme dont povoient sourdre teles trahisons et maulvaisties, car il navoit gueres de tempz que abolly et pardonne avoit a chascun quanques on luy avoit meffait, si nestoit pas a croire que son frère de Clarence ne son cousin de Warewic voulsissent penser trahison a lenthe kiug contre de sa personne; pourquoy le roy se traist en ung village la prez et se loga illec atout ses gens non gueres loingz du lieu ou estoit logie le comte de Warewic. Environ heure de myenuit vint devers le roy larchevesque dYorc, grandement adcompaignie de gens de guerre, si buscha tout liault au logis du roy, disant a ceulz qui gardoient son corpz quil luy estoit nécessaire de parler au roy, auquel ilz le nuncherent mais le roy luy fist dire quil reposoit et quil venist au matin, que lors il le orroit voullentiers. De laquele responce larchevesque ne fut pas content, si renvoia les messages de rechief dire au roy que force estoit quil parlast a luy, comme ilz le firent, et alors le roy leur commanda quilz le laissassent entrer pour oyr quil diroit, car de luy en riens ne se doubtoit. Quant larchevesque fut entre en la chambre, ou il trouva le roy couchie il luy dist prestement: "Sire levez vous," de quoy le roy se voult excuser, disant que il navoit ancores comme riens repose; mais lar- chevesque, comme faulz et desloyal quil estoit, luy dist la seconde fois: "Il vous fault lever et venir devers mon frère de Warewic, car a ce ne povez vous contrester." Et lors le roy doublant que pis ne luy en advenist se vesty et larchevesque lemmena, sans faire grant bruit, jusques au lieu ou estoient ledit comte et le duc de Clarence entre Warewic et Conventiy, ou il leur présenta son roy et seigneur souverain par luy prins en la manière dessusdite. Au roy fist le comte de Warewic grant chiere sans luy faire mal de son corpz; mais pour soy tenir sceur de sa personne lenvoia au chastel de Warewic et luy bailla la gardes qui chascun jour le menoient esbattre ou il plaisoit la entour, au moins a une lieue ou deux.

Translation:

Prepared by Livia Visser-Fuchs especially for the Northamptonshire Battlefields Society.

[Translators note: Recueil, vol. 6, bk 6, ch. 1; BnF fr. 85, ff. 277-278 (incl. half-page miniature of York beside Edward's bed and Edward meeting Warwick); BnF fr. 20358, ff. 226v-227. Fr. 20358 is a little different throughout; only important variants have been noted below.]

NB Foot notes by LVF, except where noted as by the author (GE).

When the duke of Clarence and the earl of Warwick had departed from London with all their men, they did not stop until they came to Northampton, where the *comte de Wilbie* came to meet them and handed Lord Herbert and his brother over to them. When they were brought before the earl of Warwick they started to speak to each other in very strong words, until the earl of Warwick ordered them to be taken away to die. And so these two good knights were given to the people, who stoned them to death miserably.[11]

When the abovesaid lords were dead and the men of Wales defeated, the king was informed of this and was very unhappy about it and said he had been betrayed. He had all his men armed and equipped to march against his brother the duke of Clarence and his cousin the earl of Warwick, who came towards him and were already between Warwick and Coventry when they were warned that the king was coming to meet them.

When the archbishop of York knew that the king was approaching he said to the earl his brother that he should wait for him [Edward] so that he [Edward] would have no suspicion, but that it should be found out where he [Edward] would be staying that night.

The king approached and while he rode he thought about the death of the beforesaid two knights, saying to himself that he would take revenge on his brother of Clarence

---

[11] Fr. 20358, f. 226v has: *quelz piteusement les firent morir*, who miserably put them to death.

who had so dishonoured him; and so, deep in thought and very unhappy, he rode until he came to Coventry, where he was planning to lodge. And he had indeed sent his furriers[12] there to prepare billets[13], but they discovered that the men of the North had captured the place,[14] so the said furriers were not allowed to take billets there, and they were thrown out of the town and almost killed.

Therefore they returned to the king in haste and reported to him what they had discovered, about which he was very upset, and was advised not to go any further until he had been fully informed how such treason and evil had arisen, for he had only a short while before forgiven and pardoned each of them [Warwick and Clarence] for the wrong they had done him, so there was no reason to believe that his brother of Clarence and his cousin of Warwick would wish to plan treason against his person. Therefore the king went towards a village close by and lodged there with all his people[15], not far from where the earl of Warwick was lodged.[16]

Around the hour of midnight the archbishop of York came to the king accompanied by many soldiers and knocked loudly on the door of the king's lodging, saying to his [Edward's] body guards that it was necessary that he [York] spoke to the king. They announced him, but the king had them say that he was resting and that he [York] should come back in the morning and that he would listen to him willingly then.

The archbishop was not satisfied with this answer, so he sent the messengers[17] to the king again to say that it was urgent that he spoke to him; they did so, and then the king ordered them to let him in for him [Edward] to hear what he [York] had to say, for he [Edward] had no suspicions at all.

When the archbishop had entered the room, where he found the king in bed, he immediately said: 'Sire, get up!'. The king wished to be excused, saying that he had hardly rested yet; but the archbishop, as the false and disloyal man that he was, said to him a second time: 'You have to get up and come to my brother of Warwick, and no objection is possible'.

And then the king, who suspected that worse might befall, dressed and the archbishop took him with him, without making much noise, to the place where the earl and the duke of Clarence were between Warwick and Coventry, and there he handed over to them his king and sovereign lord, whom he had taken prisoner in the way above said.

The earl of Warwick made the king very welcome without doing him any bodily harm; but to keep his person safe he sent him to the castle of Warwick and gave him

---

[12] The word in French is "fourriers". This might be read as "harbinger" or "quartermaster" in English (GE)
[13] The word in the text is "herberge" which could be read as "auberge" or Inn (GE).
[14] Fr. 20358 has: the men of the North were lodged there.
[15] The wording in the original is "gens non gueres", indicating that Edward did not have soldiers with him. Contrast this with the men who accompany York later on, who are described as "gens de guerres". (GE)
[16] Fr. 20358 ends this episode here and goes straight into the so-called *Rebellion in Lincolshire*. The text in fr. 85? continues for another few pages. This is probably due to the fact that there were Burgundian ambassadors in England (London) throughout this time and more information may have come from them.
[17] The ms has 'messages'.

guards who allowed him to exercise every day wherever it pleased him in the neighbourhood, or at least in one or two places[18].

[End of Extract]

---

[18] The phrase "au moins a une lieue ou deux" can also be translated as "up to a league or two", a league being about 3 miles.(GE)

A Brief Latin Chronicle

Being the concluding portion of a work entitled "Compilatio de gestis Britonum et Anglorum."

From "Three Fifteenth-Century Chronicles" ed James Gairdner, Camden Society, 1880.

Extract from pages 182 - 183

Anno Domini 1469, circiter festum Sancte Trinitatis, surrexit quidam, nomine Robin of Redisdale cui associati sunt multi, quasi peticionarii petentes multa corrigi in regno. Contra hos circiter festum Translacionis Sancti Thome Martiris collegit paulatim rex Edwardus exercitum, volens eis occurrere.

Et cito post cum surrexit alter, nomine Robin of Holdernes, cum complicibus suis, petens Comitatum Northumbrie restitui legitimo heredi; quem captum fecit comes pro tunc Northumbrie decollari, et dispersi sunt congregati sui.

Hoc etiam anno in vigilia Sancti Jacobi Apostoli, facto conflictu militum et belligerorum borealium contra dominum Harberd cum suis Wallensibus, ceciderunt hinc et inde multi; et dominus Harberd cum duobus fratribus suis captus est, et infra breve apud Northampton decapitatus est. Hic W. Harberd, gravissimus et oppressor et spoliator ecclesiasticorum et aliorum multorum per annos multos, hanc tandem justi Dei judicio pro suis sceleribus et nequiciis recepit mercedem. Die Sabbati proximo ante Assumpcionem beatissime semper Virginis Marie captus est Dominus de Rywans cum domino Johanne filio suo, et juxta castrum de Kelingworth pariter decollati sunt.

Translation

In the year of Our Lord, 1469, around the Feast of the Holy Trinity[1] arose several men called Robin of Redesdale, who had many followers, who petitioned for much reform in the Kingdom. Against these, around the Feast of the Translation of St Thomas the Martyr[2] King Edward gradually raised an army with the intention of confronting them.

Soon after him arose another, with the name of Robin of Holderness, with his accomplices, seeking to restore the legitimate heir to Northumbria; then he was taken captive and beheaded by the Earl of Northumberland who scattered those who were gathered with him.

---

[1] The 50th day after Easter. Easter Sunday was the 11th April in 1469, so this would be 31st May.
[2] 7th July.

Also in this year on the vigil of St James the Apostle[3] the Welsh with their leader, Lord Herbert, clashed with the host of the Northerners and many people fell on both sides; and the Lord Herbert with his two brothers was captured and within a short time beheaded at Northampton. Here W Herbert, pain, oppressor and despoiler of the Church and many others for many years finally received God's righteous judgement and received this reward for their vices and villainy. On Saturday next before the Assumption of the Virgin Mary[4] Lord Rivers and his son Lord John were taken to the castle of Kenilworth and beheaded.

[End of Extract]

---

[3] i.e. the day before the Feast of St James. This would be the 24th July, the Feast of St James being the 25th July.

[4] The Feast of the Assumption of the Virgin Mary is the 15th August. That was a Tuesday in 1469, so this would be the 12th August.

Warkworth's Chronicle of the First Thirteen Years of the Reign of King Edward the Fourth

ed J O Halliwell, Camden Society 1839

Extract from pages 6 - 8

And in the ix. yere of the regne of Kynge Edwarde, at myssomerre, the Duke of Clarence passede the see to Caleis to the Erle of Warwyke, and there weddede his doughter by the Archbysshoppe of Yorke the Erle of Warwyke brothere, and afterwarde come overe ayene. And anone aftere that, ther assig[n]ment, there was a grete insurreccyon in Yorkeschyre, of dyvers knyghtes, squyres, and comeners, to the nowmbere of xx M.; and Sere William Conyars knyghte was therre capteyne, whiche callede hym self Robyne of Riddesdale; and agens them aroose, by the Kynges commawndement, Lorde Harbarde, Erle of Penbroke, withe xliij. M. of Walschemenne, the beste in Wales, and Humfray Stafforde, with vij. M of archers of the weste countre; and as thei went togedere to mete the northemenne at a towne, there felle in a varyaunce for ther logynge, and so the Erle of Devenschyre departed from the Erle of Penbroke withe alle his menne. And Robyne of Riddesdale came uppone the Walschemenne in a playne byyonde Banbury toune, and ther thei faughthe strongly togedere, and ther was the Erle of Penbroke takene, and his brother withe hym, and two M. Walschemenne slayne, and so the Walschemen loste the felde the xxvj. day of Juylle the same yere. The names of the gentylmen that were slayne of Walsche party in the same batelle:– Sere Rogere Vaghan, knyght; Herry Organ sonne and heyre; Thomas Aprossehere Vaghan, squyere; William Harbarde of Breknoke, squyere; Watkyn Thomas, sonne to Rogere Vaghan; Yvan ap Jhon of Merwyke; Davy ap Jankyn of Lymmerke; Harry Done ap Pikton; John Done of Kydwelle; Ryse ap Morgon ap Ulston; Jankyn Perot ap Scottesburght; John Enead of Penbrokeschire; and Jhon Contour of Herforde. And of the north party ther was slayne Sere Herry Latymere, sonne and heyre to the Lorde Latymere; Sere Rogere Pygot, knyghte; James Conya[r]s, sonne and heyre to Sere Jhon Conay[r]s, knyght; Olivere Audley, squyere; Thomas Wakes sonne and heyre; William Mallerye, squyere; and many othere comyners, &c. And at that tyme was the Lorde Ryvers takene, and one of his sonnes, in the forest of Dene, and brought to Northamtone, and the Erle of Penbroke a[nd] Sere Richard Herbarde his brother were behedede at Northamtone, all iiij. by the commawndement of the Duke of Clarence and the Erle of Warwyke; and Thomas Harbarde was slayne at Brystow, &c. And at that same tyme was Stafford, that was Erle of Devynschyre but half a yere, take at Bryggewatere by the comons ther in Somerettschyre, and ther ryghte behedede. And after that the Archebysschoppe of Yorke had understondynge that Kynge Edwarde was in a vilage bysyde Northamptone, and alle his peple he reysed were fledde fro hym; by the avyse of the Duke of Clarence and the Erle of Warwyke he rode with certeyne horsmenne harneysed withe hym, and toke Kynge Edwarde, and had hym unto Warwyke castelle a lytelle whyle, and afterwarde to Yorke cite; and ther, by fayre speche and promyse, the Kynge scaped out of the Bisshoppys handes, and came unto Londone, and dyd what hym lykede. And the same yere, the xxix. day of Septembre, Humfrey Nevylle, knyght, and Charles his brothere, were takene by the Erle of Warwyke, and behedede at Yorke, the Kynge beynge present. And in the same yere [was] made a proclamacyone at the Kynges Benche in Westmynstere, and in the cyte of Londone, and in alle Englond, a generalle pardone tylle alle manere of men for alle manere insurreccyons and trespasses; and also a hole xv^{sim}. schulde be gaderyd and payed that same yere at Martyiimasse, and at oure Lady-Day in Lent after; whiche noyed the peple, for thei had payed a lytelle before a gret taske, and the xv. parte of every mannes good, &c.

[End of Extract]

Ingulph's Chronicle of the Abbey of Croyland

Translated by Henry T Riley London 1908

Second Continuation

Extract from pages 444 - 448

In the lapse of two years after this, that is to say in the ninth year of king Edward, being the year of our Lord, 1469, there arose a great disagreement between that king and his kinsman, Richard, the most illustrious earl of Warwick; which was not allayed without the shedding of the blood of many persons. The reason of this was, the fact that the king, being too greatly influenced by the urgent suggestions of the queen, admitted to his especial favour all the relations of the said queen, as well as those who were in any way connected with her by blood, enriching them with boundless presents and always promoting them to the most dignified offices about his person: while, at the same time, he banished from his presence his own brethren, and his kinsmen sprung from the royal blood, together with the earl of Warwick himself, and the other nobles of the realm who had always proved faithful to him. Accordingly, seizing this opportunity for a storm, behold! in the same year, and in the summer season, a whirlwind again came down from the north, in form of a mighty insurrection of the commons of that part of the country. These complained that they were grievously oppressed with taxes and annual tributes by the said favourites of the king and queen, and, having appointed one Robert de Redysdale to act as a captain over them, proceeded to march, about sixty thousand in number, to join the earl of Warwick, who was then in London.

The king, on hearing rumours to this effect, first had recourse to the Divine aid and to the prayers of the Saints, and, having by way of pilgrimage, first visited Edmund the Martyr, hastened to the city of Norwich. After this, he passed through Walsingham to Lynn, and thence through the town of Wisbech to Dovesdale; whence he rode, attended by two hundred horsemen, upon our embankment, and, the barriers having been opened, and all obstacles removed, at last arrived at Croyland. Here he was honorably received, as befitted the royal dignity, and passed the night a well-pleased guest. On the morrow being greatly delighted with the quietude of the place and the courtesy shown to him, he walked on foot through the streets to the western outlet of the vill, and after praising in high terms of commendation the plan of the stone bridge and the houses, there embarked together with his attendants, and setting sail, made a prosperous voyage to his castle of Foderyngey where the queen was awaiting his arrival. Having stayed here a few days only, until such time as levies of troops had assembled from all parts of the kingdom in order to assist him against the insurgents before-mentioned, he manfully prepared to march into the northern districts. The above-mentioned relatives, however, of the queen, her father, namely, and her three half-brothers, who, as we have already stated, were attached to the king's person, were in great alarm for their safety, and took refuge in different castles, some in Wales, and some in Norfolk, with the connivance, however, of the king, as it is generally said.

As for the king, when he had arrived with his army at the town of Newark, he heard that the forces of the enemy were more than threefold the number of his own troops, and, finding that the common people came in to him more slowly than he had anticipated, he turned aside and hastened with the utmost speed to his castle at Nottingham. Here he stayed a short time, intending to wait until a certain lord, William Herbert by name, who had been lately created earl of Pembroke, should come to meet him with the levies which he had raised in Wales. While, however, the said earl of Pembroke was hastening with all speed at the head of a considerable body of troops to meet the king, behold! the army of the northmen unexpectedly met him on the plain of Hegge-cote near Banbury, in the county of Northampton; whereupon, the two armies engaging, a great battle was fought, and a most dreadful slaughter, especially of the Welch, ensued; so much so, that four thousand men of the two armies are said to have been slain. The earl of Pembroke and several other nobles and gentlemen of Wales were made prisoners, and were, by order of the before-named earl of Warwick, without any opportunity of ransom, beheaded at Northampton. The truth is, that, in those parts and throughout Wales, there is a celebrated and famous prophecy, to the effect that, having expelled the English, the remains of the Britons are once more to obtain the sovereignty of England, as being the proper citizens thereof. This prophecy, which is stated in the chronicles of the Britons to have been pronounced by an angel in the time of king Cadwallader, in their credulity, receives from them universal belief. Accordingly, the present opportunity seeming to be propitious, they imagined that now the long-wished-for hour had arrived, and used every possible exertion to promote its fulfilment. However, by the providence of God, it turned out otherwise, and they remain for the present disappointed of the fulfilment of their desires.

When rumours to the above effect had now reached the king's ears, seeing that such great disgrace was, through this disaster, reflected on him, he was greatly disturbed and moved thereat. In addition to this, those who had hitherto remained firm in their allegiance to him, now became greatly alarmed, and basely deserting him by thousands, clandestinely took to flight. However, Thomas, archbishop of Canterbury, and George, archbishop of York, together with the duke of Clarence, the king's brother, and the said earl of Warwick, most duteously hastened with a large escort to hold a conference with the king, who was now left with but a very few adherents, for the purpose of soothing him in his distress. On their first arrival, in consequence of the extreme indignation which he felt, he presented a lowering countenance; but after they had fairly stated to him their intentions to remain firm in their allegiance, and had resolutely exposed the treachery of those who had adhered to him, he became more calm, and received them more freely into his favour and goodwill.

But in the meantime, while the storms of this tempest were increasing apace, you must know that we, who dwell in this island, were smitten with no small degree of terror. For by means of some spiteful enemies of ours, a most unhappy and ill-timed rumour reached the ears of certain people in the army, to the effect that those persons of whom they were in pursuit were concealed in hiding-places in Croyland, and that immense treasures were hidden in the vill and within the precinct thereof. The consequence was, that the heedless race, over ready and eager for plunder, at once declared themselves wishful, upon their return, to search our monastery and the vill with the greatest possible care; and this circumstance, together with rumour and her numerous reports, as well as the daily threats that were launched against us, caused us no small grounds for apprehension. But blessed be the Lord! who did not give us a prey unto their teeth! for, through the merits of our most holy father Guthlac, at whose tomb, each night, in Psalms and in prayers we offered up our holocausts of devout supplication, the Divine mercy dealtt graciously with us; inasmuch as, through the prudent guidance of the earl of Warwick so often mentioned, they returned from the expedition, and retired, all of them, beyond the Trent, and so, taking the shortest route, returned to their own country.

[End of Extract]

Third Continuator

Extract from pages 457 - 458

I now come to the sixth year of the reign of the said king, when Elizabeth, the eldest daughter by his marriage already mentioned, was born. This took place in the month of February, it being the year of our Lord, according to the computation of the English church, 1465, but according to that of the church of Rome, 1466. About this time, ambassadors were sent to England from Flanders, to ask the lady Margaret, sister of king Edward, in marriage for the lord Charles, the eldest son of Philip, duke of Burgundy, his father being then living. This marriage accordingly took place, and was solemnized in the month of July in the year following, being the year of our Lord, 1467. At this marriage, Richard Neville, earl of Warwick, who had for some years appeared to favour the party of the French against the Burgundians, conceived great indignation. For he would have greatly preferred to have sought an alliance for the said lady Margaret in the kingdom of France, by means of which, a favourable understanding might have arisen between the monarchs of those two kingdoms; it being much against his wish, that the views of Charles, now duke of Burgundy, should be in any way promoted by means of an alliance with England. The fact is, that he pursued that man with a most deadly hatred.

This, in my opinion, was really the cause of the dissensions between the king and the earl, and not the one which has been previously mentioned — the marriage of the king with queen Elizabeth. For this marriage of the king and queen (although after some murmuring on the part of the earl, who had previously used his best endeavours to bring about an alliance between the king and the queen of Scotland, widow of the king of that country, lately deceased), had long before this been solemnly sanctioned and approved of at Reading, by the earl himself, and all the prelates and great lords of the kingdom. Indeed, it is the fact, that the earl continued to show favour to all the queen's kindred, until he found that her relatives and connexions, contrary to his wishes, were using their utmost endeavours to promote the other marriage, which, in conformity with the king's wishes, eventually took place between Charles and the lady Margaret, and were favouring other designs to which he was strongly opposed. It is to reasons of this nature that may be attributed the overthrow and slaughter of the Welch, with their leader, William Herbert, lately created earl of Pembroke, at the battle previously mentioned, which took place at Hegecot, near Banbury: for that nobleman, at this period, had great weight in the counsels of the king and queen, his eldest son having previously married one of the queen's sisters. The queen's father also perished, Richard, earl of Rivers, already mentioned, together with Sir John Wydville, his son.

In the meantime, king Edward was taken prisoner at a certain village near Coventry, and, all his attendants being dismissed, was led thence to Warwick Castle, where he was detained in captivity. This calamity was caused by his own brother George, duke of Clarence, Richard, earl of Warwick, and his brother George, archbishop of York: and befell him in the summer of the ninth year of his reign, being the year of our Lord, 1469.

[End of Extract]

Hearne's Fragment

From "The Chronicles of the White Rose of York" ed Rev. John Allen Giles Pub James Bohn, 1843.

Extract from pages 22 - 25

Chap. 16. — Oftimes it is seen that divers there are, the which foresee not the causes precedent and subsequent; for the which they fall many times into such error, that they abuse themselves and also others, their successors, giving credence to such as write of affection, leaving the truth that was in deed. Wherefore in avoiding all such inconveniences, my purpose is, and shall be, [as touching the life of King Edward the Fourth] to write and shew those and such things, the which I have heard of his own mouth. And also in part of such things, in the which I have been personally present, as well within the realm as without, during a certain space, most especially from the year of our Lord 1468 unto the year of our Lord 1482, in the which the forenamed King Edward departed from this present life. And in witness whereof the Right Illustrious Thomas, Duke of Norfolk, Treasurer of England, as most personally present [for the most part of his flourishing age] in the house of the said right noble prince continually conversant, can more clearly certify the truth of all such acts and things, notable of memory, the which fell in his time. Of the which I am well assured, no man living may of very truth and right object to the contrary of his saying. Therefore, in avoiding all inconveniences, coloured chronicles, and affectionall histories, my purpose is to shew the truth, to avoid all ambiguity of the first motive, and original cause, wherefore Richard Neville, Earl of Warwick, withdrew himself from the amity of the 'foresaid King Edward the Fourth. Sure and of truth it is, as it appeareth in the chapters previous, the said Richard, Earl of Warwick, was sent into Normandy as Ambassador with others, whose secret counsellings betwixt the French King and him alone, brought him greatly in suspection of many things, inasmuch that his insatiable mind could not be content, and yet before him was there none in England of the half possessions that he had. For first he had all the Earldom of Warwick whole, with all the Spencer's lands; the Earldom of Salisbury, Great Chamberlain of England, Chief Admiral and Captain of Calais, and Lieutenant of Ireland; the which possessions amounted to the sum of 20,000 marks, and yet he desired more. He councilled and enticed the Duke of Clarence, and caused him to wed his eldest daughter, Isabel, without the advice or knowledge of King Edward. Wherefore the King took a great displeasure with them both, and thereupon were certain unkind words betwixt them, in so much, that after that day there was never perfect love betwixt them. Whereupon privy letters were sent into the North, into the West country, and into Wales, whereby that the Lord Herbert came to Banbury with seven or eight thousand men without any Archers. And Humphrey, Lord Stafford of Suthwicke, came out of Somersetshire and Devonshire with four or five thousand men also to Banbury; whereat their Harbingers fell at variance for lodgings, in so much that the said Lord Stafford of Suthwicke withdrew himself back ten or twelve miles. And in this season the Northern men with their captain, the Lord Latimer, which was slain there, drew nigh to Banbury to a place called Hedgecote upon the grounds of a gentleman named Clarell; of the which insurrection when the King was advertised by the Earl of Warwick, he sent out of London one Clapham with the sum of fifteen thousand men, what of household men and soldiers of Calais, whose coming was the winning of the field. For the Lord Herbert was slain, and Sir Richard, his brother, was brought to Northampton and beheaded there, and the Lord Stafford, the which came too late to the field, returned into his country, and was taken by the commons and beheaded at Bridgewater, and buried in Glastonbury. And so King Edward lost there two good captains.

Chap. 17. — In the same year those before-said Northernmen took Richard, Lord Rivers, then Treasurer of England, and one of his sons with him named Sir John Woodville, and smote off their heads: and, as some men said, it was done by the consent of the Earl of Warwick, the which was known more clearly afterwards. For a little before there was a rising in the North Country made by unnamed gentlemen, and named their captain Robin of Riddisdale, the which Insurrection was the beginning and cause of many inconveniences, as appeared soon afterwards. Howbeit they were pardoned for their Rebellion soon upon Alhalowen Tide after.

[End of Extract]

Three books of Polydore Vergil's English History, comprising the reigns of Henry VI, Edward IV, and Richard III

ed Sir Henry Ellis K.H. Camden Society, 1844.

Extract from pages 119 - 124

When Rycherd was arryvyd in his earldome of Warwicke, as we have already shewyd, he sent for his broothers, George archebisshop of York, and John marquyse Montacute ; with them, after a day or two, he commonyd of dyvers matters; and lastely, having gotten a fyt occasion to complayne uppon the king, he impartyd to them his intente, exoorting them with many woordes and reasons to joigne with him in taking king Henryes part, and to help that he might be restoryd unto his kingdome; sainge in this sort: "Yt is no lightnes of mynde, from the which I am farre of, my well beloovyd broothers, that moveth me herein, but a settlyd jugement which I may now easily make of king Henry and Edward; for he ys a most holy man, looving his fryndes intirely well, and thankfull for any benyfyt, who hath a soone, Edward by name, born to great renowme, bowntyfulnes, and lyberalytie, of whom every man may well looke for large recompense, whose care and travaile ys to releve his father in this calamytie. This on thother syde ys a man ready to offer injury, unthankfull, geaven wholly to folow sensualtie, and already shooning all honest exercyse; who resolutely maketh more honorable accownt of new upstart gentlemen than of the ancyent howses of nobylytie; wherfor ether must the nobylytie destroy him, or els he wyll destroy them. But we especyally who ar fyrst touchyd with displeasure must not put upp the matter; for I beleve yow ar not ignorant how that, after he was once settlyd in the royall seat, he began at the first secretely and than openly to envy thonor of owre howse, and, one way or other, dayly to dymynyshe the same, as thowgh he had exaltyd us unto that honor, and not we him to that royall powre and authorytie; and therfor, as concerning our late ambassage in France, we wer not accountyd uppon, to thintent that thonorable renowme which we have gotten emongest all the nobylytie of this land, partly by prowesse of owr parent, partly by owr owne travaill, might be utterly dymynsshyd, defasyd, and in no reputation".

Tharchebisshop was with these perswations easyly inducyd to be of his opynyon but so was not the marquyse, for he cowld never be movyd from the begyning to alow uppon any practyse agaynst kinge Edward; but in thende, whan therle of Warweke was promysed the ayd and assistance of many noble men, he was fynally drawen to joigne with the residew in that warre. After these thinges, therle of Warweke, being a man of most sharpe wit and forecast, conceaving before hand that George duke of Clarence was for soome secrete, I cannot tell what cause, alyenatyd in mynde from his broother king Edward, made fyrst unto him soome murmur and complaynt of the king, therby to proove him how he was affectyd; then after whan the duke dyd to him the lyke, explaning many injuryes receavyd at his broothers handes, he was the more bold to enter into greater matters, and discoveryd to the duke his intent and purpose, praying him to joigne therein. And because ther showld no suspicion of lyghtness aryse, he gave demonstration evydent how warely, perfytely, and peynfully the same had bene ponderyd and revolvyd in mynde, exhorting him also to take care and consideration of so great a cause, wherby all thinges might be throwghly provyded for, examynyd, and after a sort assuryd; fynally, after many faire promyses, he affyancyd unto the duke his doughter, which was then mareageable; by whose perswation and request the duke was overcoome, and promysyd to all thinges as he should think good.

Thus therle of Warweke, having impartyd his practyse with the duke, determynyd to make returne unto Calice, wherof as yeat he was captane, and kept his wyfe and chyldren: but to thintent that this so huge sedition, wherewith England was tossyd arid tormoylyd many yeres after, might once at the last have a begynnyng, he requyryd his brothers, tharchebysshop of York and the marquyse, to procure soome uprore to be made in Yorkshyre, anone after his departure, so that cyvill warre might be commencyd the while he was farre absent. These thinges thus determyned and his devyses approvyd, therle transportyd with the duke unto Calyce; and here, after the duke had sworne never to breake the promyse which the he had made, therle placyd unto him in maryage his eldest doughter, Isabel, betrouthyd to the duke as is before sayd ; which busynes dispatchyd, they began both two to delyberate more depely, and to conferre betwixt them selves of the maner and meanes howe to deale in this warre.

Whan in the meane time, as had bene apoynted, an huge stere arose in Yorkshyre, begun uppon a wickyd and ungodly cause. Ther was at York an auncyent and welthy xenodochye, that ys to say, an hospytall dedicatyd to St. Leonard, wher powre and nedye people wer enterteynyd, and the sicke relevyd. To this holy howse all the whole provynce dyd, for devotion sake, geave yerely certane quantitie of wheat and first fruytes of all graynes, to serve thuse of the powre, which quantyty of corne thusbandmen, by provokement and instigation of certane headesmen of therles faction, as the report went, first denyed to geave, alledging that the thinge geaven was not bestowyd uppon the powre but uppon the riche, and rewlers of the place; aftirward, whan the proctors of the sayd hospytall dyd urge the same earnestly at ther handes, they mayd an affray uppon them; by which occasion secret assembles and conspyracyes further grew, so that within few days wer gatheryd togythers abowt xv ten thowsand men, who in battayle arraye marchyd spedely towardes York. Whan the frequent fame of so great commotion came to the towne, all things wer replenysshed with a wonderus feare, the cytecyns, casting in mynd carefully what best was to be doone, contynewyd as men mutually amasyd therwith, and uncertane whether yt should be better to yssew owt agaynst the rage of this rural rowt, or to kepe the towne, and expulse ther forces from the waules.

But the marquyse, lyuetenant of that countrye for the king, delyveryd the cytie of that feere, who, taking a very fyt way for avoyding of further danger, encownteryd with the commons as they came at the very gates of the towne, wher, after long fyght, he tooke ther captane Robert Hulderne, and forthwith stroke of his heade, which when he had doone he causyd all his army to retire from the battayle, very late in the night, and withdrew them into the towne. But the people, no whyt appallyd, but rather enragyd with the death of ther captane, passing bye Yorke, whiche, withowt ordinance, and other engynes of warre they could not assalt, marchyd towardes London, myndyng to set all in uprore. And as touching that the marquyse executed the captane of the commons, whom his owne confederates in conspyracy had sturryd up, the cause semeth to have bene, for that he might therby cloke and cover his intent, ether els because he had already resolvyd in mynde to hold with king Edward, with whom (as afterward appearyd) he joignyd in mutuall benevolence.

But the king, who now began evydently to espy and conceave the secrete practyses of therle of Warweke, and of his brother the duke of Clarence, according as he had before suspectyd, after that he had intellygence, by often message and letters sent to him with all spede possyble, how that mayne multitude marchyd with banner displayed towardes London, he sent agaynst them furthwith William Harbert, whom two yere before he had created earle of Pembrowghe, with a mightie hoste of Walshemen, geaving him in charge, yf oportunyte should any wher serve, to fyght with them. The earle, using great celerytie, found the Yorkshire men encampyd not farre from Northampton, wher he also pightchyd his tents, and the next day after gave them battayll, wherin he was quikly discomfytyd.

The Yorkeshyremen, well satisfyed with this fortunate fyght, waxed soodaynly more coole, and therefor procedyd no further forward, but loden with pay drew homeward, mynding to stay whyle therle of Warweke should coome to them; who not long after, togyther with the duke of Clarence, his soon in law, hearing of that commotion, had departyd from Calyce, and was now arryvyd, muche commending the captanes of the commons, congratulatyng the victory to all the soldiers in generall, and with all dyligence preparyd an army. The king, nothing appallyd with therle of Pembrowghs late overthrow, sent him agane with suche supply as for releyf of the present necessytie he had in readynes to make head against the enemy; himself with a few foloweth after, who, that he might be preparyd at all assays, contynewally, as he went, encreasyd his forces all that he might with the people of his faction reparyng to him plentifully; he professyd openly that he went to extirp the rase of pernycious parsons. But the earle of Warweke, whan he had intelligence of thenemyes approche, sent with owt lingering unto the duke of Clarence, who was hard by with an army, that he wold bring his forces unto him, signyfying withall that the day of battayle was at hand. Uppon this message the duke reparyd furthwith to the earle, and so they both having joygnyd ther forces marchyd to a village caulyd Banbery, wher they understoode ther enemyes to be encampyd. Ther was a feyld fowghte. Therle of Pembrowghe which the was taken, all his army slane and discomfytyd. Emongest this number was killyd Rycherd earl Ryvers, father to Elyzabeth the quene, and his soone John Vedevill.

King Edward came after the same day a lyttle before night with a smaule army, and, hearing of the slaughter of his people, stayed about fyve myles from the village. Therle of Warweke returnyd with his victoryus army unto his owne towne, wher, within two days after, therle of Pembrowgh, with thother nobles taken in the conflict, was beheadyd. In the mean time they began to entreat of a pacyfycation, for the concludinge wherof messengers passyd often to and fro, from the king to therle, and from therle to the king; so that the king was now browght in hope of attonement, and by reason therof nether tooke convenyent hede to his owne affayre, nether fearyd any owtward annoyance from thennemy, as thoughe all the matter had been endyd. Wheruppon therle of Warweke, conceaving by espyalls what possybylyte he had to acheve soome fortunate exployt, approchyd the kinges camp as secretly as he could in the night, and having kyllyd the watche and ward tooke the king at unwares, whom he brought with him to Warweke, and from thence, to deceave the kinges frindes, he sent him by secret journeys in the night season to bee kept at Myddleham Castle in Yorkshire; but no place was so farre distant whyther as the fame of the kinges apprehention dyd not reache, which made many men tremble and quake for feare.

[End of Extract]

The Union of the Two Noble and Illustre Famelies of Lancastre & Yorke ("Hall's Chronicle")

Printed for J Johnson; F C and J Rivington; T Payne; Wilkie and Robinson;Longman Hurst, Rees and Orme; Cadell and Davies; and J Mawman, London 1809

Extract from pages 272 - 275

The mother of this pernicious commocion, was a charitie, or very impiety, for there was in the citee of Yorke, an olde and riche Hospitall, dedicated to Saincte Leonarde, in the whiche Almosehouse the poore and indigente people were harbored and refreshed, and the sicke and impotente persones were comforted and healed. For this good purpose and charitable intent, all the whole Prouince of Yorke, gaue yerely to this Hospitall certain measures of corne: in maner as an oblacion of the first fruites of their newe grayne, thynkyng their gyfte geuen to so holy a place, for so holy an expence, should bee to theim meritorious, and before God acceptable. Certain euill disposed persones of the erle of Warwickes faccion, intending to set a bruill in the countrey, perswaded a great nombre of husbande men, to efuse and deny to geue any thyng to the saied Hospitall, affirmyng and saiyng: that the corne that was geuen to that good intent, was not expended on the pore people, but the Master of the Hospitall wexed riche with suche almose, and his priestes wexed fat, and the poore people laie leane without succour or comfort. And not content with these sainges, thei fell to dooynges, for when the Proctors of the Hospitall, accordyng to their vsage, went aboute the countrey, to gather the accustomed corne they were sore beaten, wounded, and very euil intreated. Good men lamented this vngodly demeanure, and the peruerse people much at it reioysed, and toke suche a courage, that they kept secrete conuenticles, and priuie communicacions, in so muche, that within fewe daies, thei had made suche a confederacie together, that thei wer assembled to the nombre of. xv. thousand men, euen redy prest to set on the citie of Yorke. When the fame of this commocion and great assemble, came to the eares of the citizens of Yorke they were firste greatly astonied: but leauyng feare aside, they were in a greate doubt and vncertaintie, whether it were best for them to issue out of their walles, and to geue battaill to the rebelles, or to kepe their citie, and repulse the violence of their enemies, by the manfull defendyng of their walles and portes. But the lorde Marques Montacute, gouernor and presedent of that countrey for the kyng, did shortly put the citizens out of all feare and suspicion of inuasion, for he takyng spedy counsaill, and consideryng the oportunitie of the tyme, with a small nombre of menne but well chosen, .encountered the rebelles, before the gates of Yorke: where after long conflicte, he toke Robert Huldurne their capitain, and before theim commaunded his hed there to be striken of, and then he caused all his souldiours (because it was darke to entre into the citie of Yorke) and after their long labor to refreshe them.

Here is to be marueiled, why the Marques thus put to death the captain and ruler of the people, stirred and raised vp by hym, and the felowes of his coniuracion and conspiracie: Some saie he did it to the intent, that he would seme fautles and innocent, of all his brothers doynges, and priuie imaginations: But other affirme and saie, that he for all his promise made to his brother, was then deliberatly determined to take parte with kyng Edward, with whom (as it shall after appere) he in small space entered into greate grace and high fauor. The people beyng nothyng abashed at the death of their capitain, but rather the more eger, and fierce, by faire meanes and craftie perswasions: found the meanes to get to theim, Henry sonne and heire to the lorde Fitz Hughe, and sir Henry Neuell, sonne and heire of the Lorde Latimer, the one beeyng nephew, and the other cosin germain to therle of Warwicke. Although that these young gentlemen, bare the names of capitaines, yet they had a tutor & gouernor called sir Ihon Conyers, a man of suche courage & valiauntnes, as fewe was in his daies, in the Northe partes. And firste consideringe that they could not get Yorke, for want of ordinaunce and artilery, whiche they did lacke in dede, they determined with all spede to marche toward London, intending by the waie to reise suche a phantesie in the peoples hartes, yt they should thynke that kyng Edward was neither a iust prince to God, nor profitable to the comon welth of ye realme.

When kyng Edwarde (to whom all the dooynges of the Erle of Warwicke, and the Duke his brother, were manifest and ouerte, and wer come to that poynt, that he expected and loked for) was by diuerse letters sent to him, certified that the great armie of the Northren men, wer with all spede commyng toward London. Therefore in greate hast he sent to Wyllyam lorde Herbert, whom, within twoo yeres before, he had created erle of Penbroke, that he should without delaye encountre with the Northren men, with the extremitie of all his power. The erle of Penbroke, commonly called the lorde Herbert, was not a litle ioyous of the kynges letters, partly to deserue the kynges liberalitie, whiche of a meane gentleman, had promoted hym to the estate of an erle, partly for the malice that he bare to the erle of Warwicke, beyng the sole obstacle (as he thought) why he obteined not the wardship of the Lorde Bonuiles daughter & heire, for his eldest sonne. Wherupon he accompaignied with his brother sir Richard Harbert, a valiaunt knight, and aboue. vi or vii. thousande Welshemenne well furnished, marched forwarde to encountre with the Northren men. And to assiste and furnishe hym with archers, was appoynted Humffray lorde Stafford of Southwike (named, but not created) Erle of Deuonshire, by the kyng, in hope that he valiauntly would serue hym in that iorney, and with hym he had eight hundred archers. When these twoo Lordes were met at Cottishold, they made diligent inquiry, to here where the Northren menne were, and so by their explorators they were asserteined, that thei were passyng towarde Northampton, whervpon the lorde Stafford, and sir Richard Harbert with twoo thousande well horsed Welshmen, saied: they would go vewe and se the demeanor and nombre of the Northern men, and so vnder a woodes side, thei couertly espied the passe forward, and sodainly set on the rerewarde: but the Northren men with suche agilitie so quickly turned aboute, that in a moment of an houre, the Welshemen wer clene discomfited and scatered, and many taken, and the remnaunt returned to the armie with small gain.

 Kyng Edwarde beeyng nothyng abasshed of this small chaunce, sente good woordes to the Erle of Pembroke, animatyng and byddyng hym to bee of a good courage, promisyng hym not alonely ayde in shorte tyme, but also he hymself in persone royall, would folowe hym with all his puyssance and power. The Yorke shire menne, beyng glad of this small victory, were well cooled and went no farther Southward, but toke their waie toward Warwicke, lokyng for aide of therle, whiche was lately come from Caleis, with the Duke of Clarence his sonne in lawe, and was gatheryng and reisyng of men, to succor his frendes and kynsfolke. The kyng likewise assembled people on euery side, to aide and assist therle of Penbroke and his compaignie. But before or any part receiued comfort or succor, from his frend or partaker, bothe the armies met by chaunce, in a faire plain, nere to a toune called Hedgecot, three myle from Banbery, wherin be three hilles, not in equal distaunce, nor yet in equall quantitie, but liyng in maner although not fully triangle: the Welshemen gat firste the West hill, hopyng to haue recouered the East hil: whiche if thei had obteined, the victory had been theirs, as their vnwise Prophesiers promised them before. The Northern-men incamped themself on the Southe hill. The erle of Penbroke and the lorde Stafford of Southwike, wer lodged at Banbery the daie before the feld whiche was sainct Iames daie, and there the erle of Pembroke, putte the Lorde Stafforde out of an Inne wherein he delighted muche to be, for the loue of a damosell that dwelled in the house: contrary to their mutuall agrement by them taken, whiche was, that whosoeuer obteined first a lodgyng, should not be deceiued nor remoued. After many great woordes and crakes, had betwene these twoo capitaines, the lorde Stafford of Southwyke, in greate dispite departed with his whole compaignie and band of Archers, leauyng the erle of Pembroke almoste desolate in the toune, whiche, with all diligence returned to his host, liyng in the feld vnpurueied of Archers, abidyng suche fortune as God would sende and prouide. Sir Henry Neuell sonne to the Lorde Latimer, tooke with hym certain light horssemen, and skirmished with the Welshemen in the euenyng, euen before their Campe, where he did diuerse valiaunt feates of armes, but a litle to hardy, he went so farre forward that he was taken and yelded, and yet cruelly slain: whiche vnmercifull acte, the Welshemen sore ruled the next daie or night. For the Northren men beyng inflamed, & not a litle discontented, with the death of this noble man, in the mornyng valiauntly set on the Welshemenne, and by force of archers, caused them quickely to descende the hill into the valey, where bothe the hostes fought. Therle of Penbroke behaued hymself like a hardy knight, and expert captain, but his brother sir Richarde Herbert so valiauntly acquited hymself, that with his Polleaxe in his hand (as his enemies did afterward reporte) he twise by fine force passed through the battaill of his aduersaries, and without any mortall wounde returned. If euery one of his felowes and compaignions in armes, hud doen but halfe thactes, whiche he that daie by his noble prowes achiued, the Northremen had obteined neither sauetie nor victory.

Beside this, beholde the mutabilitie of fortune, when the Welshemen were at the very poynt, to haue obteynecl the victory (the Northernme beyng in manner discomfited) Ihon Clappam Esquier, seruaunte to the erle of Warwycke, mounted vp the syde of ye east hyl, accompanied onely with. CCCCC. men gathered of all the Rascal of the towne of Northampton and other villages about, hauyng borne before them the standard of the Erle with the white Bere, Cryenge a Warwycke a Warwycke. The Welshmen thinkyng that ye Erle of Warwycke had come on them with all his puyssance, sodaynlye as men amased fledde: the Northernmen, them pursued and slew without mercy, for ye cruelty that they had shewed to the lord Latimers sonne. So that of the Welshmen there were slayn aboue. v. M. besyde them that were fled and taken.

The erle of Pembroke, syr Rychard Herbert his brother, and diuers gentelmen were taken, and brought to Banberie to be behedded, much lamentacion and no lesse entreatie was made to saue the lyfe of Syr Rychard Herbert, both for hys goodely personage, whiche excelled all men there, and also for the noble Chiualry, that he had shewed in the felde the day of the battayll, in so muche that his brother the Erle, when he should laye doune his hed on the block to suffer, sayd to syr Ihon Conyers and Clappam, Masters let me dye for I am olde, but saue my brother, which is yonge, lusty and hardy, mete and apte to serue the greatest prince of Christendom. But syr Ihon Conyers and Clappam, remembryng the death of the yonge knyght syr Henry Neucl, Cosyn to the erle of Warwycke, could not here on that side, but caused the erle & hys brother with diuers other gentelme, to the number of. x. to be there behedded. The Northamptonshire men, with diuers of y Northernme by them procured, in this fury made them a capitayne, and called hym Robyn of Riddesdale, and sodaynly came to the manner of Grafton, where the erle Ryuers father to the Queue thenlay whom they loued not, and there by force toke the sayde erle and and syr Ihon his sonne,and brought them to Northampton, and there without Judgement stroke of their heddes, whose bodyes were solemply enterred in the Blackefreers at Northampton. When kynge Edward was aduertised of thys vnfortunate chauces, he wrote in all hast to the Shiriefes of Somersetshyre and Deuenshyre, that if they coulde by any meane take the lorde Stafford of Southwyke, that they vpon payne of their lyues, should without delay put hym in execucion, whiche accordingly to the kynges comraaundement, after long exploracion made, founde hym hyd in a village in Brentmarche, called ' where he was taken & brought to Bridgwater, & there cut shorter by the hedde. Thys was the order, manner and ende of Hegecot felde, comely called Banberie felde, foughten the morow after sainct lames daye, in the. viij. Yere of kynge Edwarde the. iiij. the whiche battaile euer synce hath bene, and yet is a cotinuall grudge betwene the Northernmen and the Welshemen. After thys battayle the Northernme resorted towarde Warwycke, where the erle had gathered a greate multitude of people, whiche erle gaue hygh commedacions to syr Ihon Conyers and other capitaynes of y North, much reioysing, that they had obtevned so glorious victory, requiring them to continew as they had begon. The king likewyse sore thrusting to recouer his losse late susteyned, and desirous to be reuenged of the deathes and murders of hys lordes and fredes, marched toward Warwycke with a great armye, and euer as he wente forwarde, his company increased, because he commaunded it to be noysed and published to the common people, that his onely entent was to destroy, and vtterly to confounde the vnhappy stocke and yll graffed generation, of suche pernicious persones, as wolde disturbe and bring in thraldome, y quiet comons and peascable people. The erle of Warwycke had by his espialles perfyt, knowlege how the kyng with his armye was bent toward hym, & sent in all hast possible to the duke of Clarece (which was not far from him with a great power) requyringe him that bothe their hostes myghte ioyne in one for as farre as he could imagyne, the tyme of battayle was very nere. The duke hearynge these newes in good order of battayle, came and encamped him selfe with the erles host. When all thynges were redy prepared to fight: by the meanes of fredes, a meane was founde how to comon of peace, for the whiche letters were writte from eche parte to other, declaring their griefes and the very bottoms of their stommackes: Herauldes spared no horseflesh in riding betwene the kyng and the erle, nor in retornynge from the Erle to the kynge: the kynge conceyuinge a certayne hope of peace in his awne imagination, toke bothe lesse hede to him selfe, and also lesse fered the outward atteptes of his enemyes, thinkyng and trustynge truely that all thynges were at a good poynt and should be well pacified. All the kvnges doynges were by espials declared to the erle of Warwycke, which lyke a wyse and politique Capitayne entendyng not to lose so great an auauntage to hym geuen, but trustyng to brynge all his purposes to a fynall ende and determinacion, by onely obteyning this enterprise: in the dead of the nyght, with an elect company of men of warre, as secretly as was possible set on the kynges felde, kylling them that kept the watche, and or the kynge were ware (for he thought of nothynge lesse then of that chaunce that happened) at a place called Wolney. iiij. myle from Warwycke, he was take prysoner, and brought to the Castell of Warwicke.

[End of Extract]

Annales, or a Generale Chronicle of England from Brute until the present yeare of Christ 1580

Collected by IOHN STOW Citizen of London.

Printed at London by Ralphe Newberie, at the assignement of Henrie Bynneman

Extract from pages 722 - 723

The Duke of Clarence went to Calleis, & there wedded Isable one of ye daughters to ye Earle of Warwike. Sir Iohn Coniers knight, Robert Hilliard, who named himself Robin of Ridsedale, & other, gathered an host of. 20000. mē in ye North, against whō K. Edward sent W. Herbert late made Earle of Penbroke, with. 18000. Welch men, and Humfrey Stafforde of Southroike, late made Earle of Deuon wt 6000. good archers, which ij. Erles falling out for lodging in ye towne of Bābery, .Hūfrey Stafford departed wt his power, whereby W. Herbert & Richard Herbert his brother were ouercome & taken by thē of the North &. 5000. (saith Hall) of the Welchmen slaine in a plaine called Danes more, néere to ye towne of Edgecote, iij. miles frō Babery, ye 26. of July. The men of name slaine of ye Welch party, were sir Roger Vaughā knight, Henry ap Morgan, Tho. ap Richard Vaughā Esquier, W. Herbert of Brecknocke Esquier, Watkin Thomas son to Roger Vaughan: Inā ap Iohn ap Meridik, Dauy ap Iankin ap Limorik, Harrisdon ap Pikton, Iohn Done of Kidwelly, Rice ap Morgā ap Vistō, Iankin Perot ap Scots Burg, Iohn Euerard of Penbrokeshire, Iohn Courtor of Hereford. The Northrē men of name slain were, sir Henry Latimer sonne & heire to ye Lord Latimer, sir Roger Pigot Knight, Iames Coniers sonne & heire to sir Iohn Coniers Knight, Oliuer Awdley Esquier, Tho▪ Wakes sonne & heire to W. Mallerie Esquier: Richard Woodvile Lord Riuers, wt Iohn his sonne, were takē in ye forest of Dene & brought to Northamptō, where they with sir W. Herbert & Richard his brother were all iiij. beheaded, by ye cōmaundement of ye duke of Clarence, & the Erle of Warwike. T. Herbert was slaine at Bristow. Humfry Stafford was by the commōs taken at Bridgewater, and beheaded. King Edwarde was taken at V[...]nar, a village beside Northampton, by ye archbishop of Yorke, & brought to Warwicke Castell, & thence to Yorke, from whence by faire promises he escaped, & came to London.

[End of Extract]

The Annales of England[1]

By John Stow

Printed 1603

Extract from pages 700 - 701

This Duke of Clarence went to Caleis, and there wedded Isabell one of the daughters of the Earle of Warwicke. Sir Iohn Coniers knight, Robert Hilliard who named himselfe Robin of Ridsdale, and other, gathered an host of 2000 men in the North against whom King Edward sent W. Herbert late made Earle of Penbroke with 18000 Welchmen, and Humfrey Stafford of Southwike late made Earle of Deuon,with 6000.good archers, which two Earles falling out for lodging in the towne of Banbery, Humfrey Stafford departed with his power, whereby G.Herbert and Ric.Herbert his brother were overcome and taken by them of the North, and 5000. (saith Hall) of the Welchmen slain in a plaine called Danes more nere to the touone Edgecote, three miles from Banber, the 26. of July. The men of name slaine of the Welch party were Sir Roger Vaughan knight, Henry ap Morgan,T ap Richard Vaughan Esquire, W. Herbert of Brecknocke Esquire, Watkin Thomas sonne to Rog.Vaughan. Inan ap Iohn ap Meridick, Dany ap lankin ap Limorik, Harrisdon ap Pikton, Iohn Done of Kidwelly, Rice ap Morgan ap Vlston, lankin Perot ap Scotes Burg, Iohn Euerard of Penbrokeshire, Iohn Courtor of Hereford. The Northmen of name slaine were, sir Henry Latimer sonne and heire to the Lord Latimer, Sir Roger Pigot knight, Iames Coniers sonne and heire to sir Iohn Coniers knight, Oliuer Audley Esquire, Th. Wakes sonne and heire to W. Mallory Esquire: Richard Woodville Lord Riuers with Iohn his sonnewere taken in the forest of Deana, and brought to Northampton, where they with Sir W Herbert and Richard his brother were all foure beheaded by the commandement, of George Duke of Clanrence and the Earle of Warwicke. Th Herbet was slain at Bristow, T Stafford was by the commons taken at Bridgewater and beheaded. King Edward was taken at Ulnay, a village before Northampton by the Archbishop of Yorke, and brought to Warwicke Castell and thence to Yorke, from whence by faire promises he escaped and came to London.

[End of Extract]

---

[1] The Annales of England was based on the previous publication, expanded and amended up to the date of publication, in this case 1603. In respect of the campaign and Battle of Edgcote there is a small but significant difference.

Bibliography

This bibliography is brief as it does not include those works which have had extracts reprinted in the Sources appendix. It has also been the intention in preparing this work to rely mostly on primary sources, and only turn to modern works to determine how the story has developed through various historians telling of the story.

Modern Studies

Bicheno, H	Blood Royal	Head of Zeus Ltd 2015
Barnard, F P	Edward IV's French Expedition of 1475	OUP 1925
Brooks, R	Cassell's Battlefields of Britain & Ireland	Cassell's 2005
Coveney, T	Heraldic Banners of the Wars of the Roses, (3 Volumes A-H, H-R, S-Y)	Freezywater 1997
Curry, A	Agincourt, A New History	The History Press 2010
Evans, H T	Wales and the Wars of the Roses	Sutton 1995
Haigh, P A	The Military Campaigns of the Wars of the Roses	Sutton 1995
Haigh, P A	"...where both the hosts fought..."	Battlefield Press 1997
Hicks, M	Warwick the Kingmaker	Wiley-Blackwell 2002
Hicks, M	The Wars of the Roses	Osprey 2003
Ingram, M	The Battle of Northampton 1460	Northampton Battlefields Society 2015
Lander, J R	The Wars of the Roses	Sutton 2007
Oman, C	Warwick the Kingmaker	Macmillan 1891
Ramsay, J	Lancaster and York: A Century of English History	Clarendon, 1892
Ross, C	Edward IV	Yale 1974
Seward, D	The Wars of the Roses	Robinson 2002
Scofield, C	The Life and Reign of Edward the Fourth, Volume 1	Fonthill Media 2016
Weir, A	Lancaster & York: The Wars of the Roses	Pimlico 1998

Journal Articles

Dockray, K R	The Yorkshire Rebellions of 1469	The Ricardian Vol 6, No 82 (Dec 83)
Lewis, B	The Battle of Edgecote or Banbury (1469) through the eyes of contemporary Welsh poets.	Journal of Medieval Military History: Volume IX: Soldiers, Weapons and Armies in the Fifteenth Century ed Curry A and Bell A R. Boydell and Brewer, (2011)
Lewis, W G	The Exact Date of the Battle of Banbury, 1469	Bulletin of the Institute of Historical Research, LV (1982b)

Antiquarian Works

Baker, G	History and Antiquities of the County of Northampton, Volume 1	London 1822-1830
Beesley, A	The History of Banbury	London 1841
Morton, J	The Natural History of Northamptonshire	London 1712
Poulson, G	The History and Antiquities of the Seigniory of Holderness, Volume 2	Hull & London 1841
Timmins, S	A History of Warwickshire	London 1889

Internet

Guto'r Glyn.net: http://www.gutorglyn.net/gutorglyn/index/

The Battlefield Today

Luckily the area that the battle took place in is readily accessible to anyone who doesn't mind a bit of a walk. Despite many centuries of farming and "improvement" the shape of the ground where the battle took place (at least according to this interpretation) is largely untouched, with the biggest changes, if any, being to the hydrology of the area.

The battlefield is on farm land, and any attempt to visit the location should firstly respect that, and follow the Countryside Code in the case of animals and gates. Luckily there are public footpaths that allow access to the area, and provide a very pleasant afternoon's walk through the South Northamptonshire countryside. The main starting locations for the walk can be found off the A361, the modern road that links Banbury to Daventry and has mislead so many earlier historians. Trying to follow Banbury Lane from Northampton is not an easy task as much of it is no longer open to vehicular traffic.

At the time of writing the Griffin Inn in Chipping Warden is a good place to either start or end your walk if you want a drink and or a meal. As you are walking across countryside on Bridle Paths and permitted footpaths - which includes the Battlefields Trust's "Battlefield Trail" that links Edgehill, Cropredy Bridge and Edgcote - it won't hurt to take the relevant Ordnance Survey map with you (No 206 - Edge Hill & Fenny Compton). From Chipping Warden take the Jurassic Way footpath up towards Edgcote village and House. This will take you across the Cherwell and you will be able to see how the river has been managed in the time after the battle. By the way, as you cross the river, to your left the wooded area contains "Warriors Wood", where grave pits have possibly been found. The Church in Edgcote village, St James, has no connection to the battle and the tombs in it relate to the family that held the land after the Clarells. The church is normally locked, but access is possible by prior arrangement (you'll need to search the internet for the keyholders, - they are currently on the "Northamptonshire Surprise" website).

From Edgcote do not follow the Battlefield Trail to your left (you'll come back that way) but go to the right up the road, before turning off to the left on to the Jurassic Way at the Edgcote Drive cottages. This will take you up onto Edgcote Lodge Farm Hill after a steepish path. The Haigh theory battlefield will be to your left at this time.

At the top of the hill you will pick up the Battlefield Trail to your left. Follow this along the crest (through where Ramsey placed the battle) and you will come to Edgcote Lodge Farm. The area you have walked along is where Herbert's camp was situated, and where he was "shot off" the hill by the rebel archers. The land to your right front is Danes Moor (not the land to your right rear, which is the race course). The path goes round the back of Old Spinney on the end of the hill, and descends into Danes Moor. This is farm land which may contain crops, so please stay on the pathway.

In the middle of Danes Moor the trail branches to the left, and takes you to the stream where most of the fighting is thought to have taken place. It is a sad, overgrown, little thing now, but was more substantial in the past.

Crossing over the stream - it is culverted - the trail takes you up on to the "East Hill". Looking back from here gives the best view of the battlefield, and enables you to appreciate both armies' positions. The trail goes over the crest, and meets up with the "Millenium Way" at a "crossroads". Going straight ahead takes you to Culworth, to the right is the route the rebels took to get into position from Thorpe Mandeville.

Turn to the left on the Battlefield Trail and head North towards Trafford Bridge. Danes Moor spinney to your left is the location of the Bicheno theory battlefield. As the trail emerges out onto the road you will find the Battlefield Trust information board. Follow the road to the left and cross over Trafford Bridge. The bridge does not date from the time of the battle. This road, by the way, is the "Welsh Road" droving route.

Taking the road will bring you down to a signpost pointing to your left, marked Battlefield Trail, which will bring you back to Edgcote village where you originally turned to the right, and you can follow the same path back to Chipping Warden.

You can also access this circular walk from Wardington. When we visited the pub it served a good pint of beer, but wasn't serving food on that day, so check beforehand if you want to eat. Pick up the public footpath to the North East of the village from the lane connecting Wardington and Edgcote. This will take you up to the hill crest where you can join up with the Battlefield Trail. This approach gives you a better look at Ramsey's proposed approach march, if you think that is important.

The last time my Northamptonshire Battlefields Society colleague, Phil Steele, and I did the walk was in May, and it was a very pleasant ramble, but some bits can be muddy (you are on farm land after all). In spring and summer there is quite a bit of foliage, and for the more hardy of you there might be benefits in walking the ground when the trees and hedges are a bit barer. Today's landscape probably has more woodland on it than in 1469, when most was being used for ridge and furrow farming.

Northamptonshire Battlefields Society

Northamptonshire Battlefields Society was formed in February 2014 in order to promote and preserve the county's battlefields heritage. The inaugural meeting took place at the Northampton Marriott Hotel which is situated on the edge of the registered 1460 Battlefield.

We bring together the local community, members of the public, historians, wargamers, archaeologists, re-enactors and academics from all over Britain, Europe and the US, but especially Northamptonshire, who all share a passion for Northamptonshire's rich but apparently largely forgotten history. Our aim is to engage in further research and to promote and protect the heritage that survives today, an aim that has lead us to set up the "Save our Eleanor Cross" campaign.

We have also worked as consultants with both Northampton Borough Council to develop a plan for the interpretation of the 1460 battlefield (including stands and information panels) and with Delapre Abbey Preservation Trust for their new battlefield visitor centre at Delapre Abbey.

Our patrons are Earl Charles Spencer, Lord Charles Fitzroy of Grafton Regis, Lord Boswell of Aynho, Charles Chetwynd-Talbot, 22nd Earl of Shrewsbury, whose ancestor fought and died at the 1460 battle and world famous author of historical novels, Bernard Cornwell.

NBS has won several awards for our work on Northamptonshire's Battlefields including:

- The Battlefields Trust's Presidents Award for outstanding contribution to battlefield preservation and interpretation,
- The International Guild of Battlefield Guides for significant contribution to the craft of battlefield guiding and the wider Military History community and
- The NN4 Eight Community Group for the protection of the 1460 Battlefield.

We hold monthly meetings throughout the year, except for August and December, at the Delapre Golf Centre, Northampton, normally on the last Thursday of the month and have a wide range of high calibre expert speakers from all over the UK. Please see our Facebook page for details. Meetings are free to fully paid up NBS members or £7.50 to non-members on the door (this is the cost as at 2019. The charge is set at half a full year's single membership fee). We also take our mobile exhibition stand to a number events around the country including major wargames shows, where we will normally be found with the Society of Ancients. Our e-newsletter is published on a quarterly basis. Called "The Wild Rat" (named after the banner that the men of Northampton marched under when they were summonsed to join a Royal Army) it reports on all of our regular meetings and keeps members up to date with issues of concern and the Society's activities.

The Main Aims and Objectives of the Society are to:

a) Advance public education through the promotion, encouragement, development and dissemination of knowledge of the battles of Northampton and their landscapes, as well as the associated wars and warfare;
b) Undertake and support research into the battles and their landscapes, the associated wars and warfare and the publication of the results of such researches;
c) Encourage the identification, protection and preservation of such sites
d) To organise talks and courses that will provide members and the general public with relevant information, knowledge or skills to pursue individual or group research;
e) To mount a programme of activities on topics relevant to the battlefields in the locality, the County of Northamptonshire and further afield;
f) To arrange and lead guided walks of the battlefields;
g) To mount exhibitions of an historical nature;
h) To create and maintain an internet presence including a Northamptonshire Battlefields Society website, Facebook page and Twitter feed;
i) To publish a range of books, leaflets and resource materials relating to the history of the battles and battlefields;
j) To act as a resource for material and information for schools, libraries, media, museums etc;
k) To extend any of the above and develop additional activities as opportunities arise.
l) To advise and assist the appropriate authorities and to co-operate with other bodies having similar interests

Membership is open to all, and the membership year runs from January to December.

Printed in Poland
by Amazon Fulfillment
Poland Sp. z o.o., Wrocław